3

E²

USING THE POWER OF

ETHICS AND ETIQUETTE IN AMERICAN BUSINESS

PHYLLIS DAVIS

Ep
Entrepreneur Press

Editorial Director: Jere L. Calmes
Cover Design: Beth Hansen-Winter
Production and Composition: Eliot House Productions

This publication is designed to provide accurate and authoritative information in regard to the subject matter covered. It is sold with the understanding
that the publisher is not engaged in rendering legal, accounting or other professional services. If legal advice or other expert assistance is required, the
services of a competent professional person should be sought.

Library of Congress Cataloging-in-Publication Data
Davis, Phyllis, 1949–
     E2—using the power of ethics and etiquette in American business/by
Phyllis Davis.
          p.   cm.
     Includes bibliographical references and index.
     ISBN 1-891984-77-2
          1. Business ethics—United States—Handbooks, manuals, etc. 2.
Business etiquette—United States—Handbooks, manuals, etc. I. Title: Using
the power of ethics and etiquette in American business. II. Title: E squared—
using the power of ethics and etiquette in American business. III. Title.

HF5387.5.U6D38 2003
174'.4—dc21   2003041951

Printed in Canada

10 09 08 07 06 05 04 03   10 9 8 7 6 5 4 3 2

Table of Contents

Acknowledgments, xi
Foreword by Tom Silveri, CEO
*   and president of DBM Inc., xiii*
Introduction, xv

SECTION I
FIRST AND LASTING IMPRESSIONS

CHAPTER I   *The Handshake* 3
Scenario Setup: Effecting an
    *Un*memorable Handshake, 5
Checklist: The Handshake, 7
Case Study 1. Using the Handshake, 8
Chapter Summary, 10

CHAPTER 2   *Power Impressions* 11
Scenario Setup: Making an Entrance, 12
Case Study 2. Seamless Entries, 12
Scenario Setup: Making a Powerful
    First Impression in 30 Seconds, 13
Case Study 3. Making Those First 30 Seconds Count, 15
Chapter Summary, 16

CHAPTER 3   *The Business Card* 17
The Seven Most Important Items
    on Your Business Card, 18
Uses and Purposes of the Business Card, 18
Scenario Setup: Presenting Your Business Card, 18
Scenario Setup: Receiving a Business Card, 20
Case Study 4. The Business Card Exchange, 21
Chapter Summary, 22

CHAPTER 4   *Introductions* 23
Scenario Setup: Making a Business Introduction, 24
Ten Rules for Business Introductions, 24
Checklist: Age and Importance During Introductions, 26
Scenario Setup: Those Awkward
    Moments of Introduction, 27
Case Study 5. Introductions, 28
Chapter Summary, 29

CHAPTER 5   *Listening and Hearing Skills* 31
Four-Step Formula for Active Listening, 32
Checklist: Active Listening, 33
The Benefits of Effective Listening, 34
Active Hearing Tips, 34
Case Study 6. Listening and Hearing, 35
Chapter Summary, 37

CHAPTER 6   *Communication Skills* 39
Benefits of Effective Communication, 40
The Four Channels of Basic Communication, 40
The Visual Communicators, 42
The Kinesthetic Communicators, 42
The Auditory Communicators, 43
The Auditory Digital Communicators, 44
Case Study 7. Channels of Communication, 44
Chapter Summary, 46

CHAPTER 7   *Discussion and Décor* 47
The 30-Day Rule, 48
Checklist: Making Small Talk in
    Business Dining Situations, 48

Checklist: Making Small Talk in Business Settings, 49
Telephone Small Talk, 50
Case Study 8. Small Talk and the 30-Day Rule, 50
Decorating Your Personal Office Space, 51
Suggestions for Decorating Your Office Space, 51
Case Study 9. Personal Office Décor, 52
Chapter Summary, 53

CHAPTER 8 *Professional Appearance* 55
The Businesswoman, 56
This Woman Makes Sense, 57
The Businessman, 63
Men's Apparel Questions Answered, 64
Chapter Summary, 70

CHAPTER 9 *Getting the Job* 73
Scenario Setup: Your Job Interview, 75
Leesa McElroy's Interview Tips, 77
Your Resume, 79
Chapter Summary, 79

SECTION II
RISING IN THE CORPORATION

CHAPTER 10 *Moving Up the Corporate Ladder* 83
Creating Your Game Plan, 84
Case Study 10. Your Strategy for Success, 87
Using Your Soft Skills to Raise Your Personal Profile, 87
Checklist: Your Personal Visibility Campaign, 88
Case Study 11. Raising Your Profile, 92
Your Personal Publicity Campaign, 92
Case Study 12. Highlighting Your
    Diplomacy Skills and Humanity, 93
Chapter Summary, 94

CHAPTER 11 *Office Protocol During Delicate Situations* 95
Cubicle Behavior, 95
Checklist: Dealing with Irritating Behaviors, 96
Case Study 13. Constructive Cubicle Advice, 97
What About *Your* Habits?, 97

Dealing with Sarcastic People, 97
Case Study 14. Dealing with Sarcastic People, 98
Death of a Co-Worker—Funeral Etiquette, 99
Checklist: Acknowledging the Death of a Co-Worker, 99
Case Study 15. Expressing Sympathy and Support, 100
Personal Phone Calls, 101
Case Study 16. Managing Personal Phone Calls, 101
Yawning, 101
Case Study 17. If You Get Caught Yawning, 102
Bluntness, 102
Checklist: Avoiding Bluntness, 103
Case Study 18. Communication vs. Bluntness, 103
Chapter Summary, 104

CHAPTER 12 *Business Meetings*. 105
Meeting Leader Techniques, 106
Ten Techniques for Leading a Successful
    Business Meeting, 107
Scenario Setup: Leading a Successful Meeting, 109
The Code of a Good Meeting Leader, 112
Checklist: When You're Attending a Meeting, 113
Chapter Summary, 114

CHAPTER 13 *Mastering Corporate Politics* 115
Ten Steps for Winning at Office Politics, 116
Case Study 19. Showing Honor, 116
Case Study 20. Turning Enemies into Allies, 117
Case Study 21. Showing Respect, 119
Case Study 22. Agree and Redirect, 121
Case Study 23. Remain a Private Professional, 123
Case Study 24. Hold Confidences, 124
Case Study 25. Act Decisively, 125
Case Study 26. Remaining Loyal to Your Company, 126
Case Study 27. Knowing Your Company's History, 127
Case Study 28. Offering Encouragement, 127
Chapter Summary, 128

CHAPTER 14 *Diplomacy and Personal Accountability*. 129
Delivering Compliments, 130
How and When to Give Praise, 130

Receiving Compliments, 131
Two Behaviors that Kill Compliments, 131
Behaviors that Encourage Compliments, 132
Case Study 29. Giving and Receiving Compliments, 132
How to Handle Criticism, 133
Criticism from an Office Associate, 134
Checklist: Dealing with Inner-Office Criticism, 134
Case Study 30: Dealing with Abusive Criticism, 135
Humor and Joke Telling, 136
Case Study 31. Using Quotations for
    Levity in the Workplace, 137
Dealing with Frustration or Anger, 138
Checklist: Managing Your Frustration and Anger, 138
Case Study 32. Keeping Your Cool, 140
Office Gossip, 140
Case Study 33. What to Do with Office Gossip, 142
Chapter Summary, 142

SECTION III
CLIENT SERVICES

CHAPTER 15 *Networking*. 145
Eight Good Reasons to Network, 146
Find a Room to Work, 147
If You Can Answer YES to Any or All
    of These Questions, Then GO, 147
The Four Secret Keys for Attending
    Networking Group Meetings, 148
Checklist: Creating Your Successful Networking Plan, 149
Checklist: Working the Room, 150
Scenario Setup: Working the Room, 153
The Networking Thread of Follow-Up, 155
Checklist: Following up the Networking Thread, 155
Chapter Summary, 157

CHAPTER 16 *Techno-Ethics:*
    65 Tips for Etiquette Related to Technology. 159
Electronic Mail, 160
Facts about Facsimiles, 164
Telephone and Voice-Mail Manners, 165

The Horrible Hold Button, 166
Tone, Diction, Timing, and Grammar on the Phone, 167
Cell Phone Manners, 167
Pager/Beeper Manners, 169
Chapter Summary, 170

CHAPTER 17 *Client Protocol* 171
Codes of Conduct for Setting an Appointment, 172
Case Study 34. Making an Appointment, 172
Codes of Conduct for Punctuality, 173
Case Study 35. Punctuality Conduct, 173
Codes of Conduct for Waiting Rooms, 174
Scenario Setup: Waiting Room Conduct, 174
Scenario Setup: Greeting Your Appointment
    and Making Rapport-Deepening Comments, 176
Scenario Setup: Getting to Your Point
    and Concluding Your Meeting, 177
Scenario Setup: Following Up Your Meeting, 178
Chapter Summary, 178

CHAPTER 18 *Choreographing the Business Dinner* 179
Scenario Setup: Fine Dining and Business, 180
Scenario Setup: When You're Someone's
    Guest at a Restaurant, 186
Checklist: Dressing for Dinner, 187
Chapter Summary, 188

CHAPTER 19 *Gift Giving, Conventions,*
    Events, and Social Occasions 189
Business Gift Giving, 190
Seven Things to Know About Business Gift Giving, 190
How Much to Spend, 192
What to Give, 192
Office Party Etiquette, 193
RSVP, 193
Buffets, Barbeques, and Pool Parties, 194
Scenario Setup: Attending Buffets,
    Barbeques, and Pool Parties, 194
Checklist: Planning for a Business Conference,
    Convention, or Banquet, 196

Scenario Setup: Attending a Conference Banquet, 197
Scenario Setup: Being an Invited Guest at a Business
    Associate's Wedding, 199
Chapter Summary, 201

SECTION IV
DIVERSITY AND DISABILITY IN THE WORKPLACE

CHAPTER 20 *Diversity in the Workplace* 205
    Religious Sensitivity in the Workplace, 206
    Checklist: Respect for Others' Religion, 207
    Gender Sensitivity Toward
        Women in the Workplace, 207
    Checklist: Respect for the Businesswoman, 208
    Ethnic Sensitivity in the Workplace, 209
    Checklist: Welcoming Cultural Diversity, 210
    Sexual Orientation Sensitivity in the Workplace, 211
    Checklist: Respecting Sexual Orientation, 211
    Chapter Summary, 212

CHAPTER 21 *Disability Sensitivity in the Workplace* 213
    Suggestions for Working with a Person
        Who Has a Disability, 216
    Chapter Summary, 217

SECTION V
ETHICS IN THE WORKPLACE

CHAPTER 22 *Personal Code of Ethics* 221
    Personal Code of Ethics for _____, 222
    Chapter Summary, 223

CHAPTER 23 *Corporate Code of Ethics* 225
    Advice from the Council of Better Business
        Bureaus Inc.: Establishing an Ethical Business, 226
    Developing Your Company's Code of Ethics, 228
    Code of Ethics for the Texas Independent
        Automotive Association, 229
    Chapter Summary, 229

SECTION VI
ETIQUETTE THERE, THEN, AND NOW

CHAPTER 24 *History of Etiquette* 233
A Manners Time Line, 235
Chapter Summary, 239

CHAPTER 25 *Global Etiquette* 241
When You're in Japan, 243
When You're in Hong Kong, 243
When You're in India, 244
When You're in Thailand, 244
When You're in Argentina, 245
When You're in France, 246
When You're in Germany, 246
When You're in Italy, 247
When You're in Saudi Arabia, 248
When You're in China, 248
When You're in England, 249
When You're in Mexico, 250
Chapter Summary, 250

A Note from the Author, 253
Suggested Reading List, 255
Index, 257

Acknowledgments

I'D LIKE TO THANK COLLE DAVIS, MY WONDERFUL AND LOVING husband, whose fingerprints are on every page of this book. Colle Davis is the finest executive business coach of our time (www.mycoach.com). He is an old-world debonair gentleman whom I respect and admire. He is my Cary Grant.

I offer a sincere thanks to Tom Silveri, CEO and president of DBM Inc. for his support for this book and its place in the world of business. I'd also like to extend my gratitude to my friend Vanessa Castagna, CEO and president of J.C. Penney Company, for her faith in me and encouragement to bring my message to the world.

I'd also like to thank my editor and champion, Jere Calmes at Entrepreneur Press; my book producer, Karen Billipp at Eliot House Productions; my beloved brother, Phil Estes; my brilliant and funny media trainer, Nancy Greystone; my friend and literary agent, Wendy Keller of Forthwrite Literary Agency, my friends Dee Ground, Karen Norris, Peter Brusso, CEO, Infocard.cc, Brian Weiner, and everyone at City Club on Bunker Hill in Los Angeles, California and the Century City Chamber of Commerce in Los Angeles, California.

Thanks to Letitia Baldridge, Dale Carnegie, Peggy and Peter Post, Judith Martin, Julia Cameron, and those whose life's work has inspired me and millions of others.

A special thanks to Mack Gaston (rear admiral in the U.S. Navy, retired, and vice president of Global Government Solutions, Electronic Data Systems, E.D.S.); Alvin S. Rudisill Ph.D.–D.Hu.L, (university chaplain emeritus, distinguished emeritus professor, professor of medical ethics in the Schools of Religion and Medicine, University of Southern California); Rodney Cole (Men's Wearhouse); Sherry Maysonave (author of *Casual Power*); Kathie Snow (author of *Disability Is Natural*); The Council of Better Business Bureaus; Leesa McElroy; Melissa Balaban Esq. (Employment Practices Solutions); Fran Pomerantz of The Pomerantz Group; Mark Abelsson; Georgette Bennett Ph.D. (president of The Tanenbaum Center for Interreligious Understanding); Billy E. Vaughn Ph.D. (president and founder of The Diversity Training University International LLC); and The Texas Independent Automotive Association.

To all those who contributed to the success of this book and all those who will benefit from their support, I say, "Thank you."

Also, in loving memory of Ruth Carter Stapleton.

Foreword

IN THE MAD SCRAMBLE TO ACHIEVE THE GOALS WE'VE SET FOR ourselves and our loved ones in today's new economy, it's time we came to a screeching halt to examine what it's costing our relationships and reputations. Haste is indeed making waste, and we're feeling the cost in our soured economy and tattered corporate and personal images. That which we learned at our mother's knee, or later on in hallowed halls of our alma maters and religious institutions, seems to have lost all relevance. Our moral compasses seem to be pointing nowhere.

If you can't look to public or business leaders as models of behavior or to the benchmark institutions they represent for guidance in matters of critical importance to our stability and well-being, where can you look? Phyllis Davis would answer, "In the mirror," or she might borrow a quote from Harry Truman and remind the reader that "the buck stops here." In her book, *E2*, she marries ethics to etiquette and mandates that we attend the wedding and live happily ever after by getting back to basics and modeling for others what we have known all along but have allowed ourselves to forget—that ethics and courtesy are not optional but critical and essential to our welfare and our happiness.

As the CEO of a human resources consulting firm with hundreds of offices around the world, I travel a great deal of the time, and I see that the challenge is not an "American" anomaly; it is a global reality. Technology has improved our lives but has allowed us to avoid the personal touch that was such a part of the fabric of our corporate lives and the factor so fundamental to our success. *E2* could not have arrived at a more opportune time.

Phyllis' sophisticated primer guides us through those unsure moments of our complex, stressful, fast-paced, and depersonalized corporate lives, helping us to put one foot in front of another in putting our best foot forward. From the handshake and entrance into a corporate setting to the handling of delicate matters requiring great sensitivity, Ms. Davis is at our side every step of the way. Corporate politics, diplomacy, diversity, ethics, etiquette, and entertaining are all covered in this important guide. Thank you, Phyllis. The world will be a better place thanks to you and *E2*.

—Tom Silveri,
CEO and president of DBM Inc.

Introduction

I<small>T'S AN UNDENIABLE FACT. T</small>HE <small>BASIC RULES FOR</small> civility in American business have changed. Personal accountability has been questioned and challenged from boardroom ethics to mail-room security across the country in companies large and small. In October 2001, Enron announced a $1 billion, loss and during that same month, an anthrax letter was found in U.S. Senator Tom Daschle's office. In those dark days of our nation's history, Americans were still reeling from the terrorist's attacks that had occurred a month earlier on the World Trade Center in New York City. We could not see the faces of any of our enemies, and we felt suckerpunched and justifiably frightened. Clearly, we didn't know who we could trust. Seemingly overnight, we became a nation in search of heros and heroines; there was a unanimous cry demanding a return to order, evidence of public and personal trust, demonstrations of honesty, and displays of goodwill.

This book addresses the immediate need for the recognition and restoration of a higher level of American business ethics and

Novus Ordo Seclorum

Latin phrase inscribed under the pyramid on the back of the American one-dollar bill. This translates closely to "A new order has begun," or "A new order of the ages."

etiquette. Many of the business skills introduced in this book have never before been written down. Instead, they have been passed on by way of trial-and-error experience as well as oral explanations and extensive exposure to corporate culture. It is a thought-provoking read for top-level executives, human resource managers, departmental supervisors, or those in job transition. It's also mandatory reading for corporate-bound college graduates to educate themselves about corporate behavior before they jump into the job market. This book provides savvy tools for relationship management, best-case customer service scenarios, and advice for those who want to build internal and external corporate loyalty.

On July 30, 2002, in the East Room of the White House, President George W. Bush signed The Sarbanes-Oxley Act of 2002. This new law demands corporate responsibility and insists on high levels of honesty and business practices. In President Bush's public address on the day of the bill-signing, he sent a clear warning to all dishonest corporate leaders by saying, "The era of low standards and false profits is over; no boardroom in America is above or beyond the law." On the other hand, he assured the many ethical and respectable business executives, "This law says to honorable corporate leaders: Your integrity will be recognized and rewarded, because the shadow of suspicion will be lifted from good companies that respect the rules."

Yes, the rules have changed. After the corporate and political crises that have occurred in this country, there is now a higher order of expectation for all citizens engaged in American business to protect our American way of life. There is an urgent need for all those engaged in business to exhibit a visible demonstration of their manners, diplomacy, and personal integrity.

Top-down management and corporate responsibility can alter the course of America's future. The challenge to choose the higher road is up to each individual.

May the day come when you'll choose a path that will continue to build the strength of your company, this country, and your own personal integrity—and may this day be such a day for you.

FIRST AND LASTING IMPRESSIONS

The Handshake

CREATING A SUCCESSFUL COMPANY requires the cooperation of all individuals employed by that company to accept a high level of personal accountability. Sounds reasonable enough, doesn't it? After all, we all know that businesses are built as a collaborative effort with the time and talents of their employees toward a common goal. Then why are some companies within the same industry more successful than others? It's a question worth considering since employers need to fill their ranks with talented and loyal employees, and consumers need to be reassured they're making the right choice by doing business with you and your company. Any company who can

> "Give me a stock clerk with a goal and I will give you a man who will make history. Give me a man without a goal and I will give you a stock clerk."
>
> —JAMES CASH PENNEY, FOUNDER OF J.C. PENNEY COMPANY, 1875–1971

successfully accomplish both of these objectives will create a competitive edge in today's marketplace.

Many companies have a public, corporate code of ethics available to their consumers. Corporate ethics could be defined as a company's promise or pledge to their consumer agreeing to deliver their product or service and to stand behind what they sell. However, in order for a company to make that promise, all employees in that firm should know their company's code of ethics, be willing to declare their own personal code of ethics and agree to hold themselves to the highest levels of professional behavior in order to accomplish their company's objectives. Anything less than an employee's complete understanding and acceptance of that agreement diminishes the company's competitive edge and ultimate success.

> "Even if I knew that tomorrow the world would go to pieces, I would still plant my apple tree."
>
> —MARTIN LUTHER, CHRISTIAN MONK, 1483–1546

It's an open discussion in many sectors of business today: "How can today's business leaders enforce ethics within their company?" And the answer is clear: "It must come from the top level of management down to every employee in the company." It is also the complete responsibility of today's corporate leader (or should be) to model ethics within their own companies, their industries, and their communities. If all of today's CEOs and presidents were to openly insist on high standards of corporate and personal ethics for themselves and all of their management teams, it would set the example for their entire companies to follow.

During these troubled times, it's a tragedy that many think the term "corporate ethics" is considered an oxymoron because of corporate corruption at the top levels of Enron, WorldCom, and others. The actions of a few corporate leaders have shaken consumer confidence and employee loyalty to the core. The only way American businesses can reclaim and rebuild that confidence is to demonstrate their own levels of civility by encouraging and educating their employees in proper and professional business decorum. Education requires training, mentoring, and encouragement. In light of the recent fall of business leaders, it's time for a new and enlightened learning curve to resonate with the needs of today's business. It's not too late to restore a high sense of values, security, and self-esteem in American business dealings. In the famous last words of Todd Beamer, the passenger who died in the crash of United Airlines Flight 93 on September 11, 2001, "Let's roll." In his honor, and in honor of all those before and after him who love this country, and for the privilege of free enterprise, let's roll up our sleeves and get to work. Together, we can change the future of the world. Ready? Let's go to work.

> If your handshake is done properly, it should be quite unmemorable.

Throughout this book, you will find sections titled "Scenario Setups," and they will take you by the hand and walk you through a virtual learning experience for a specific topic by providing you with a visual tutorial for rapid learning. Let's start with the most basic exercise for making a positive impression, the business handshake. If you think you already know everything there is to know about the handshake, then you might be surprised to learn a few new pointers. The handshake is a theatrical pleasantry that's (hopefully) warm and friendly and, if it's done properly, quite *unmemorable*. The cold truth is, if anyone remembers your handshake, it's because it's weak and clammy or because you've got a painful vise grip. Your handshake is your opportunity to give a favorable impression of your personality and your character. It's meant to create a human connection during an introduction and reinforce that connection when you bid farewell.

Scenario Setup: Effecting an Unmemorable Handshake

> ➤ Always stand during a handshake unless you are elderly, ill, or physically disabled.
> ➤ After standing, offer the person whose hand you're shaking an eyebrow flash and create focused eye contact

> Dr. Desmond Morris notes that the eyebrow flash is innate and used instinctually by people all over the world when they greet one another.

before initiating or responding to the offer of a handshake. Renowned primate expert and psychologist Dr. Desmond Morris notes that the eyebrow flash is innate and used instinctually by people all over the world when they greet one another. It is a small movement (1/6th of a second) that involves a quick raising and then lowering of both eyebrows during a greeting. This gesture leaves both eyes momentarily unprotected and gives the person you're greeting an unconscious message that you trust them.

➤ Place the web (between thumb and index finger) of your right hand into the web of the other person's right hand and then *very slowly* wrap your fingers around the other person's hand and flatten your palm against his or her palm while slightly bending your thumb over on the back of his or her hand. Apply two or three slow pumps. A slow handshake is considered sincere. Don't rush. Take your time.

➤ Engage in a warm clasp (not too weak or hard) and avoid cupping your right hand. Men often shake a woman's hand by cupping the right hand to avoid their normal firm grip. Any woman will tell you she prefers a firm, warm grip over a cupped one since the latter can be painful if it crushes the ring on her right hand.

➤ Talk while you're shaking hands. Exhibit a pleasant facial expression and speak instead of waiting until the handshake has concluded. If you remain silent and do not appear sincere or pleasant, your handshake could be misconstrued as apathetic or even aggressive. In fact, try saying the other person's name first (if you know it) before giving yours. For example, "Hello Bill. It's nice to meet you. I'm Pat Patrick."

➤ Avoid turning a person's wrist and hand sideways so yours is on top and his or her is underneath in a less dominant position. This is considered highly aggressive and is always inappropriate.

➤ Make sure your right hand is dry, not moist.

➤ Never involve your left hand in a handshake. Placing it over the handshake or on the left arm or elbow of the other person is considered insincere and often called "The Politician's Handshake" or "The Preacher's Handshake."

➤ If you'd like to add an extra degree of warmth to your handshake, allow yourself to bow slightly to the other person. Do this by bending almost imperceptibly from your waist. This may or may not be your style, and it's not required, but it's a warm and ingratiating gesture.

➤ You'll never know about your handshake until someone gives you feedback. Shake hands the way you normally do with three people and ask for their critiques. Is it too strong? Too fishy? Are you a cupper? Once you've completed this experiment, shake each person's hand again using the suggestions in this chapter and see if they like your new and improved method.

✔ Checklist: The Handshake

You will find sections titled "Checklist" throughout this book. These sections provide you with the facts, rules, and nuances of a specific topic, and you can always refer back to any checklist to refresh your memory.

> If you meet a senior-ranking officer in your company, wait for him or her to initiate the handshake.

The first checklist is designed to instruct you on the appropriate use of the business handshake.

❑ Wait for a senior-ranking officer in your company to initiate the handshake when you meet.

❑ Wait for the other person to initiate the handshake when you walk into that person's private office.

❑ Rise from behind your desk and initiate a handshake when someone—your guest—walks into your office.

❑ Wait for a woman to extend her hand to you when you're not sure whether she wants to engage in a handshake. The vast majority of contemporary businesswomen shake hands routinely. However, some women of certain ages and areas of the country have never learned to shake hands with strangers and may be reluctant to do so.

❏ You don't need to shake a person's hand each time you see him or her during the workday unless there's a specific reason to do so.

❏ When an invited guest comes to your office for a business meeting, initiate a handshake and introduce yourself and those around you.

❏ If you are being introduced to someone by a third person, be quick to initiate the handshake at the beginning of your introduction. If you're introducing yourself, initiate the handshake as you begin introducing yourself or when the other person begins the introduction.

CASE STUDY 1

Using the Handshake

You will also find sections titled "Case Study" throughout this book. They will help you quickly check your understanding of a topic before you move on to the next subject. You will find Issues for your consideration followed by the solutions to those issues. The first Case Study offers you self-test questions to see if you are proficient in the handshake.

ISSUE

If you are seated and someone approaches and offers to shake your hand, what should you do?

SOLUTION

You should rise from your chair and shake the person's hand. Never shake their hand from a seated position.

CASE STUDY 1, CONTINUED

ISSUE

If you are considered a junior officer in your company and approach a senior officer, do you offer to shake hands?

SOLUTION

No. You wait for the senior officer to extend his or her hand and then extend your right hand for the handshake.

ISSUE

If you walk into the office of a person you do not know, do you offer to shake hands?

SOLUTION

No. You enter the office slowly (with a pleasant expression on your face) and wait for the person to offer to shake your hand; only then do you extend your hand for the handshake.

ISSUE

If an invited guest (who doesn't know anyone) enters a business meeting, do you offer to shake hands?

SOLUTION

Yes. To make your guest comfortable, be the first to extend your hand and introduce yourself and anyone who is standing close to you.

ISSUE

Does a businesswoman initiate a handshake to a man or another woman?

SOLUTION

Yes. Today's professional businesswoman offers to shake hands with anyone except a senior executive; in that case, she waits for the executive to initiate the handshake.

||||||||||||||||||||||||||||||||

CHAPTER SUMMARY

★ Smile when you shake hands, always wait for a higher-ranking person to offer to do it first, and never involve your left hand. Pump your hand two or three times very slowly and do not grip too tightly or lightly.

★ Even though the rules for business etiquette should apply equally to both men and women, there are a few exceptions. If you question whether a woman will shake hands with you, wait for her to offer her hand first.

★ Women dislike a cupped handshake and prefer a warm, slow, and sincere one.

★ Initiate a handshake when someone enters your office and remember, always stand first.

Power Impressions

THERE IS A PREMEDITATED WAY TO MAKE A dignified entrance into your office each day. Most offices try to create an ambience of formality to inspire businesslike behavior in their associates and customers.

Be aware that making a business entrance into an office is quite different from making a social entrance into a party or the home of a friend. By definition, social situations are for the purpose of joviality, relaxation, and enjoyment. Your business entrance should be professional and quiet, seamless and understated, so that you assimilate into the office and avoid disturbing the work in progress. You want to avoid drawing too much attention to yourself and those involved in business activities.

Scenario Setup: Making an Entrance

This Scenario Setup applies to making an entrance into your own office, a client's office, or the office of a potential customer.

➤ Prepare yourself before you cross the threshold of the doorway by standing erect and adjusting your clothing if necessary.

➤ Make a quiet entrance. If you're on your cell phone, ask the person on the line to excuse you for a moment before you walk through the office. If you must travel far from the doorway of the building to an office, say you'll return the call when you have some privacy.

➤ Wear a pleasant expression on your face and enter the room slowly, calmly, and confidently.

➤ Avoid making eye contact with people who are working or who are on the phone. Instead, allow your eyes to gaze over the tops of people's heads as you make your way through the work area.

➤ Keep your hands to yourself. Don't touch anything on anyone's desk as you pass by.

➤ If someone says hello, respond quietly and quickly and move on through the office.

➤ When entering a room to attend a meeting, choose one or two people to stand with and talk to instead of moving around and chatting with many people. Allow yourself to move slowly and quietly into a group and try not to demand attention when joining a conversation in progress.

CASE STUDY 2

Seamless Entries

ISSUE

You're called to your boss' office on the 12th floor. As you step off the elevator of the 12th floor, what would you do to make a seamless entrance?

CASE STUDY 2, CONTINUED

SOLUTION

You would walk quietly through the maze of offices leading to your boss' office, nodding and saying a private hello to a few people without disturbing the business in progress. When you're traveling from the elevator to your boss' office, don't touch anything on anyone's desk. If you must use your cell phone before arriving at your boss' office, find a private area so you won't disturb the work in progress. Don't answer your cell phone during your meeting with your boss (more on Techno-Ethics in Chapter 16).

ISSUE

How do you make an entrance into a meeting that is about to begin?

SOLUTION

As you enter the meeting room, choose one or two people to stand with for a few moments instead of moving from person to person. After joining a group, spend more time listening than talking until the meeting begins.

Scenario Setup: Making a Powerful First Impression in 30 Seconds

You can create a favorable first impression through a series of easily duplicable actions that can be accomplished with some rehearsal and practice. People like being around those who look like them, act like them, and have similar ideals and mannerisms; experiment with these skills to create a memorable first impression.

> ➤ After meeting someone and shaking hands, make your first comment to and about the other person, not about yourself. People love the sound of their own name, so repeat it and say something like, "Tony, it's nice to meet you. My name is Ray Jones."
> ➤ Most men are more comfortable when you're standing at a 90- to 120-degree angle from them rather than standing face to face with them.

- Women enjoy standing with their shoulders parallel (torso squared).
- Gentlemen, to make a woman comfortable, stand face to face with her. Women, to make a man comfortable, should angle their torso.
- Wear the industry-appropriate dress (or uniform) of your company with pride and respect.
- When meeting a superior in your company for the first time, say something relevant and avoid talking about yourself. For example, "Mr. Black, it's an honor to meet you and to be a new employee of this great company." Yes, this comment may sound a bit solicitous, but you are acting in a way that indicates your respect for him and his position in the company.
- After you've made your comment to Mr. Black, say nothing else and wait for him to respond to you. If he does, then answer his question or address his comment. If he doesn't, he may have a lot on his mind and may not want to engage in a conversation with you at that moment.
- Mirror Mr. Black's body gestures very slowly and carefully. If he leans forward, then you lean forward. If he leans back, then you lean back. This takes practice, or you'll get caught in the act of mirroring him. Subtle mirroring puts him at ease, but he won't know why he feels this way.
- Mirror and match Mr. Black's pace in conversation. If he speaks slowly, you speak slowly. If he speaks quickly, you speak quickly. Again, people are at ease around others who act and think like them.
- As you say good-bye to Mr. Black, don't mention yourself first by saying "I enjoyed meeting you." Instead, focus on him: "It was a pleasure meeting you," or "Thank you for taking a moment of your time to speak with me."
- As you depart, if Mr. Black does not offer to shake your hand again, simply thank him, smile sincerely, and leave with a pleasant expression on your face. He may end your brief encounter thinking, "I like that new employee," but not know why.

Making Those First 30 Seconds Count

ISSUE

Say you're new in a company. What is the first thing to say to a senior-ranking officer when you meet?

SOLUTION

Say something about her or him or the company. Don't begin your conversation by mentioning anything about yourself such as, "I'm Pat Smith. I'm a new employee in accounting." Instead, make your comment relevant to the officer. For example, "Mr. Black, it's an honor to meet you and be a new employee of this great company. My name is Pat Smith."

ISSUE

After you've greeted your senior-ranking officer, what do you say next?

SOLUTION

Don't say anything else. Give them a chance to respond to your statement or ask you a question.

ISSUE

If you want to make a great first impression and the person you're speaking to is smiling while talking, do you also smile while you talk?

SOLUTION

Yes. Always match the person's smile to create an immediate sense of rapport in 30 seconds. In essence, you become a mirror of them.

ISSUE

In business, do most men like to stand face to face with squared shoulders facing another person's shoulders?

SOLUTION

No. Men are generally comfortable in business settings when their torsos are at a 90- to 120-degree angle to each other.

CASE STUDY 3, CONTINUED

ISSUE

If a woman is addressing another woman in business, what stance makes the two most comfortable?

SOLUTION

Women are generally comfortable facing each other directly (torsos squared) in both business and social situations.

ISSUE

If a man wants to put a woman at ease in a business setting, what is one thing he can do?

SOLUTION

He can stand directly in front of her with his torso squarely facing her.

ISSUE

If a woman wants to put a man at ease in a business setting, what is one thing she can do?

SOLUTION

She can stand at a 90- to 120-degreee angle to his torso.

CHAPTER SUMMARY

★ When making an entrance, walk quietly into your office in the morning; don't disturb people, and listen more than you talk.

★ To make a positive and lasting first impression on others, dress appropriately for the occasion, comment on them and not yourself, and observe and mirror their style. When speaking to a male, angle yourself; when speaking to a woman, you may square your shoulders with hers.

The Business Card

> "We are what we repeatedly do. Excellence then, is not an act, but a habit."
>
> —ARISTOTLE, GREEK PHILOSO-
> PHER, 384–322 B.C.

HANDLE YOUR BUSINESS CARD AS IF IT were made of a very thin piece of mirrored glass. It's a reflection of who you are in the business community, just as other people's cards reflect who they are. All business cards should be given and received with a formality that eludes most Americans.

Your business card is more than paper and ink; it's a personal extension of you and your company. It may come as a surprise to you, but your name is the least important point on your card. The recipient wants to know what company you work for and your official title within that company.

The Seven Most Important Items on Your Business Card (in order of importance)

1. Your company's name and logo.
2. Your company's Internet home page address (if you have one).
3. Your title within the company; this should indicate your hierarchy and job function (for example, vice president of sales).
4. What city you're in. Include your location address (street, city, state, zip).
5. Your phone number. Avoid including your cell-phone number unless you're never in your office.
6. Your office e-mail address.
7. Your name.

Uses and Purposes of the Business Card

Your business card serves the following purposes *besides* the exchange of contact information. It

- attaches to a business letter or company brochure
- can be included with a bouquet of flowers intended for business purposes
- attaches with a note in a business gift
- can be includes with a business thank-you note or business-related greeting card.

Scenario Setup: Presenting Your Business Card

➤ Prior to arriving at a business event or meeting, place a dozen business cards in perfect condition in a card holder that carries no more than a dozen cards. This card holder can be a slender metal or leather case. These cards should have no smudges or folded edges, and nothing handwritten on them or scratched out and corrected. Place that card holder somewhere convenient in your clothing. If you're a man, that means in your right jacket or trouser pocket (if you're right-handed) or the left

---

Present your card type side up,
facing the other person.

---

breast pocket of your jacket. If you're a woman, it means in your right pocket (if you're right-handed) or an easily accessible place in your handbag.

➤ When someone asks for your card, present it to them with the type side up, facing them, so they can easily read it.

➤ Don't randomly ask people for their card. Wait until you have developed a comfort level with a person and there's a *specific reason* for asking.

➤ Never ask senior executives for their cards whether they are in your company or another one. If a lower-ranking person asks a senior-ranking officer for a card, the higher official may say she or he doesn't have one; the truth is, the executive may not want to hand out the card and be contacted. Senior officers will ask for someone's card if they want it, and in exchange, may offer one of theirs.

➤ Avoid passing your cards out to anyone who will take them since casual giving reduces you and your card's value. Try to avoid joining in random card exchanges at networking events. You've probably had the experience of arriving back at your office with a pocket or purse full of cards and not knowing whose card belongs to whom; you throw away the batch because they have no significance.

➤ Don't lay any business card on any table where food is present. Instead, put all cards in your pocket or purse. Granted, networking events promote the exchange of business cards, but placing them on a dining table is still considered below the bar of proper business practices.

➤ If you're seated at a large, round dining table at a business conference with nine strangers, and the person sitting next to you asks for your card, discreetly take one from your holder and privately give it to the person out sight of the others seated at the table.

➤ If someone across the round table asks for your card, don't pass it through other people's hands to deliver it. Instead, get up and walk around the table and hand it to the person, or say you'll provide it after dinner.

Scenario Setup: Receiving a Business Card

➤ When someone gives you a card, try to accept it with two hands and study it for two or three seconds. Make at least one comment about the card's logo design, the company or its location, or the person's job title or function.

➤ After you've finished this brief discussion, place the card in a convenient place (separate from your own business cards) so you can take it out again in a moment and make a brief notation on it about the person. This will help you recall the person when you return to your office. For example, "His grandmother plays tournament golf," or "She knows about our health-care products."

➤ Gentlemen, if you receive a business card from someone, don't put it in your wallet and return your wallet to your back pocket. This shows poor form and, in some cultures, is considered a supreme insult to the card's owner.

➤ Try to receive a card graciously even when someone forces it on you and you don't want it. You can always throw it away at the office. However, if someone you have no intention of calling tries to force a card on you and insists that you call, kindly say you'd rather not take the card.

Make at least one comment
about some feature of a
person's card.

CASE STUDY 4

The Business Card Exchange

ISSUE

You're attending a conference, and you'd like to have the card of someone there. How do you get it?

SOLUTION

Create an opportunity to chat with this person and a specific reason to ask him or her for the card; then you can contact later via e-mail or regular mail. However, if the person is a senior-ranking officer within your or another company, you must first establish rapport with the person and develop a specific reason for her or him to ask you for your card in hope that the executive will offer you a card.

ISSUE

What do you do when you're at a conference and people are passing stacks of their cards around a table during dinner?

SOLUTION

Don't put a stack of your cards in the mix. Save them for those who have a specific reason for wanting them.

➢ Once back at the office, carefully go through each card and place those you want to keep in your card file; you may also want to record vital information from a few of them in your organizer. Then throw the rest of them away. If you think some of the cards are particularly important and want to continue your contact with the people, drop them an e-mail or a handwritten note saying you enjoyed meeting them at the cocktail party. Always include your business card with a handwritten note, even if you've already given the person one.

||||||||||||||||||||||||||||||||||||

CHAPTER SUMMARY

★ When giving a business card, make sure it's immaculate and present it type-side up; study a card given to you for two seconds and then comment on it; don't hand out your card randomly; don't let it touch a dining table; and wait for a senior-ranking person to ask for your card.

★ Business cards accompany business letters, gifts, flowers, thank-you notes, and greeting cards.

★ Avoid receiving a card, placing it in your wallet, and putting your wallet in your back pocket.

Introductions

THE MOST IMPORTANT THING TO REMEMber about making formal introductions is that a person of a higher rank or status *receives* the introduction of someone of lower rank or status. This is accomplished by using the name of the higher-ranking person first.

This section may require some rehearsal since the rules regarding business introductions differ from those of social introductions.

> "Meeting Franklin Roosevelt was like opening your first bottle of champagne; knowing him was like drinking it."
> —WINSTON CHURCHILL, PRIME MINISTER OF GREAT BRITAIN, 1874–1900

Business introductions are based on hierarchal status in the areas of business, politics, academics, and organized religions. There is one person on Earth who receives introductions from all people, and that is the pope, the head of the Roman Catholic Church. This honorary formality is out of

> A person of a higher rank or status receives the introduction of someone of lower rank or status. This is accomplished by using the name of the higher-ranking person first.

respect for the office of pope since there has been a continuous line of since A.D. 32.

Formal business introductions are less common today than they once were, but it's still important to know when and how to make standard introductions in your business life. To learn more about formal introductions within governments, academic circles, faith-based organizations, or the military, check out one of the many books on the subject at your public library. There is also a reading list of reference works at the back of this book.

> "Mistakes are the portals of discovery."
> —JAMES JOYCE, IRISH AUTHOR, 1882–1941

Scenario Setup: Making a Business Introduction

➤ Always use the name of the most important person in the introduction first. In the following case, you're introducing your office manager (Brenda Jones) to your brother (Stephen Estes): "Brenda Jones, I'd like you to meet Stephen Estes," or "Brenda Jones, may I introduce Stephen Estes."

➤ You might also insert a bit of information about Stephen Estes, such as, "Brenda Jones, I'd like for you to meet my brother, Stephen Estes."

➤ If you'd like your brother to know Brenda Jones is your office manager, after you've made the introduction, turn to Stephen and say, "Brenda is the manager in our office."

Ten Rules for Business Introductions

1. You must know the status and hierarchal rank of the two people you're introducing and then use the name of the

higher-ranking person first. For instance, if you are introducing an entry-level employee to a senior level executive
in your company, the executive is the more senior person
and his or her name should be used first.

2. Know the first and last names of both people you're introducing.

3. Pronounce each person's name correctly.

4. Know some piece of pertinent information about each
person that will bring relevance to the introduction. For
example, after someone's name you might add, "Joe works
in the New Jersey branch of the office." This added tag line
gives the two strangers a chance to begin a casual and
relaxed conversation.

5. Know a bit of information about an individual's rank,
title, or job function. For example, "Joe Joseph is the vice
president of purchasing for Soles and Laces Shoe Store."

6. Use an individual's formal, academic, or political title
before their last name. For example, Doctor Brown,
Judge Green, Reverend Gray, Professor White,
Congresswoman Black, Senator Blue. When individuals
have formal titles, do not use their first names unless they
invite you to do so.

7. You don't need to use the terms Mr., Mrs., or Ms. when
making casual business introductions unless you're introducing a person of an advanced age to someone much
younger. If older people want you to use their first names,
they'll invite you to do so.

8. If you're making a more formal introduction between a
senior-ranking executive in your company and a person
without any business rank or dignitary status, it's a
supreme courtesy to the senior executive to call them Mr.,
Mrs., or Ms. when commenting on them in their presence
to the person without rank. For example, "Joe Green, I'd
like you to meet my uncle, Sam Pickle, from Sacramento."
Then turn to Uncle Pickle and say, "Mr. Green is the president of our company."

9. When you are formally introduced to someone, repeat the person's name back to them. This is considered a diplomatic and gracious gesture and is not necessary in all business introductions, but it can make a lasting impression. For example, after being formally introduced to Mike Tunnell, you might say, "Mike Tunnell, it's a pleasure to meet you." Repeating the name gives you a chance to memorize and practice pronouncing it correctly. Remember, people love to hear the sound of their own names.

10. Name tags do not take the place of introducing yourself at a business conference. Once you're engaged in a conversation of any duration, wait for an opportunity, initiate a handshake, and say "Hello. I'm Jim Sloan from the marketing division of the Balloons and Batteries in Detroit."

✔ Checklist: Age and Importance During Introductions

❑ *During a formal introduction between a client and an officer in your company*, the client always trumps the rank and status of the officer. For example, "Mike Miller, I would like you to meet Alice Green, our company's CEO." At this point, you can turn to Alice Green and say, "Mike Miller is the vice president of sales for Nickels and Dimes Stores based in Atlanta."

❑ *During a formal introduction between a person of advanced age (who is generally retired from corporate life) and a younger person*, the older person generally trumps the younger one. For example, "Mr. Leavett, I would like you to meet our new account executive, Marsha Miller." Remember to use Mr., Mrs., or Ms. when introducing a person of advanced age.

❑ *If you're introducing a senior executive in your company to the mayor, governor, or a noted dignitary, the dignitary's status trumps that of your senior executive.*

Scenario Setup: *Those Awkward Moments of Introduction*

➤ Say you're standing with a client (Bill Blue), and a dozen people you know in your company approach you; you do not need to introduce Bill Blue to each person. Instead, just make a few introductions. You might say to the entire group, "I'd like to introduce you all to Bill Blue, who is the vice president for Plumbing and Feathers in Fort Worth, Texas. They're a new client with us." A few people may step forward to introduce themselves and shake Bill's hand, others may just smile and offer him a nod or a greeting such as, "Hello" or "Welcome."

➤ Forgetting someone's name can be embarrassing, especially when the person remembers yours. Don't ignore the person or wait for him or her to make an introduction to someone in a group. Instead say, "I'm sorry, my memory is slipping; please remind me of your name," and then wait for the person to tell you.

Saying "I can't remember your name" is a poor choice since it insults and further devalues the person whose name you've forgotten; it's better to blame your own memory than minimize the other person's importance. You might also tell an anecdote about the person that draws him or her into your conversation and asks for a name. For example, "I know you, but my memory has failed me. I remember you have two golden retrievers and live on a lake near Seattle, and yet, your name has slipped my mind." The person will tell you his or her name. Don't make a big deal out of forgetting the name; just continue with your introduction.

CASE STUDY 5

Introductions

ISSUE

You're introducing Alice Green (CEO of your company) and Frank White, an accountant in your company's Pasadena office. How do you do it?

SOLUTION

"Alice Green, this is Frank White, an accountant in our Pasadena office." If Frank White is unaware of the fact that Alice Green is CEO of the company, it's appropriate to follow your introduction by saying, "Alice Green is the CEO of our company." Note: Both Alice Green and Frank White shake hands (two or three slow pumps of their right hands) as you begin introducing them.

ISSUE

You are introducing Alice Green (CEO of your company) to a new client, Bill Blue, vice president of Plumbing and Feathers in Fort Worth, Texas. How do you do it?

SOLUTION

"Bill Blue, I'd like you to meet Alice Green, our CEO." Then turn to Alice Green and say, "Bill Blue is vice president of Plumbing and Feathers, and a new client with us from Fort Worth, Texas."

ISSUE

How do you introduce your client (Bill Blue) to an accountant within your company?

SOLUTION

Bill Blue, this is Wanda White. Wanda's an accountant in our Pasadena office." Then add a tag line such as, "Wanda, Bill is the vice president of Plumbing and Feathers, and he's a new client from Forth Worth, Texas."

CHAPTER SUMMARY

★ The basic rule for making a formal introduction is that a person of a higher rank or status receives a person of lower rank or status. This is accomplished by using the name of the higher ranking person first.

★ Use formal titles (doctor, reverend, professor, etc.) during introductions.

★ A client always trumps a company officer in importance during an introduction.

★ A person of advanced age generally trumps a younger person in importance during an introduction.

★ A dignitary trumps a senior-ranking executive in your company.

Listening and Hearing Skills

THIS MIGHT SURPRISE YOU: WHEN OTHER people are talking to you and you're listening carefully, you're the one in control of the conversation. By practicing and perfecting the skills of *active listening,* you can guide and direct any business conversation in the direction you'd like it to go.

Our busy culture doesn't allow enough time for people to finish their thoughts and be heard. Many people avoid speaking to one another because they feel no one cares about what they have to say, and they fear being ignored or embarrassed.

Make a conscious decision to listen. With time and practice, you can improve your reputation and advance your professional life. If you observe politically adroit business leaders, you'll see they have learned to quiet their mind when someone is speaking to them. They have perfected the ability to use their own verbal and nonverbal language skills to encourage others to keep talking. They don't interrupt. They don't finish other people's sentences or ignore direct questions. They became leaders by knowing how to get *you* to talk to them and give them the information they need to make wise company decisions.

Once you've learned the skills for active listening and hearing, people will come to trust you. If you fail to listen and hear, they may not trust what you say, even if it's the truth. They will trust you if you've learned how to actively listen and speak in a way that makes them *want* to believe whatever you're saying is the truth. By exhibiting mannerisms that indicate you hear what people are saying, that you see them, and appreciate the value they represent, you are creating the foundation for successful relationships essential in today's business climate.

If you listen long and well enough, people will tell you everything you want to know. Your job is to listen and use well-rehearsed skills to get other people to talk.

Four-Step Formula for Active Listening

A key component for effective leadership is gaining knowledge and then positioning that information effectively in a timely manner to create positive results. As you listen to people, begin to ask them questions and encourage them to continue talking by providing them prompts and probing questions until they've told you everything you want or need to know.

1. *Acknowledge.* Remain neutral when people are speaking to you and use prompts to keep them talking: "Yes, I see," or "Uh huh," or "That's interesting."

2. *Repeat.* Sum up what the speaker has said to show you're listening: "What you're saying is, your department has not made the transition to the new system. Is that correct?"

3. *Validate.* Tell the speaker you see their point of view: "It seems as if this has been a difficult transition for your department."

4. *Reflect.* Bring together the important points the person made by recapping their comments. "Let me make sure I understand what you've said. If your department had been assigned three more employees on your team by July 1st, you would have been able to implement the new system. Is that right?"

✔ Checklist: Active Listening

❑ Avoid stealing comments from others to talk about your own experience on the subject.

❑ Practice a steady visual focus and avoid allowing your eyes to dart around the room.

❑ Stick with one subject.

❑ Avoid starting sentences with "I."

❑ Listen when someone is speaking to you instead of listening to your own thoughts.

❑ Allow the person who's speaking to you the time to sum up what they're trying to say.

❑ Listen and avoid giving unsolicited advice.

❑ Keep both your hands still. Avoid fidgeting and playing with your cell phone, beeper, appointment book, or personal data organizer. Don't tap your pencil, play with your hair, turn and twist your jewelry, or flip your necktie.

❑ Agree or nod occasionally when someone is speaking to you. Avoid arguing with the speaker to show you're right. Once you become defensive in any way, the person will stop giving you valuable information.

❑ Answer questions as directly as possible. However, if you're not in a position to share confidential information, say you can't give a direct answer because it's confidential.

❏ Listen to the content of what is being said and avoid judging the comments of the speaker by critiquing their accent, use of words, sentence structure, or inflection.

❏ Wait until the speaker finishes before you speak. Be patient.

The Benefits of Effective Listening

> "Listening is a magnetic and strange thing, a creative force. The friends who listen to us are the ones we move toward. When we are listened to, it creates us, makes us unfold and expand."
>
> —KARL MENNINGER, M.D., EMINENT PSYCHIATRIST, 1893–1990

Learning to listen to what people are saying without listening to your own silent voice of judgment, cynicism, lack of trust, or boredom about what's being said to you is vital to your success. When you learn this skill, you'll find others will give you information that will enable you to make wise business decisions. Careful listening inspires people to trust you because your careful listening inspired them to give you information, and that means you'll learn more about a variety of topics.

The more you listen to others, the easier it will be for them to solve their own issues or problems without any input from you. Once they've worked through their issues, they'll give you much of the credit for their new clarity and wisdom. As you become viewed by others as a person who listens carefully, when you do speak, others will listen attentively in order to hear what you have to say. People are hungry to be heard. By listening, you are giving them a great gift. They won't know exactly why, but people will like you more.

Active Hearing Tips

Few people hear you when you speak to them; instead, most have developed the sloppy habit of *selective hearing* and *divided attention.* Even during face-to-face conversations, people may look like they're listening and understand what you're saying, but the sad truth is, they're really only sorting for words, details, or phrases that interest them. The result of sloppy hearing skills is poor long-term memory and second-rate communication, which are inferior models both for relationship management and business development.

Here are a few tips for active hearing that inspire confidence so people will speak to you openly and answer your questions.

> "We have two ears and one mouth so that we can listen twice as much as we speak."
>
> —EPICTETUS, PHILOSOPHER, A.D. 50–138

- Blink slightly slower than normal when others are speaking. This gives the speaker a visual indication that you are carefully processing what they are saying.
- Make a conscious decision to listen. Act as if your job depends on it. The truth is, it may.
- Maintain good eye contact but don't stare the person down.
- Nod very slowly when appropriate.
- Lean slightly toward the speaker.
- Make occasional encouraging comments that indicate you're listening and want the speaker to continue. For example, "Please, go on," or "Tell me more," or "What you're telling me is important for me to hear. Continue."
- Set aside your own judgments, beliefs, attitudes, and thoughts of your own appearance long enough to allow someone else to speak to you.

CASE STUDY 6

Listening and Hearing

ISSUE

A senior-ranking officer in your company tells you a new policy is being considered for implementation in your department because of a problem. You don't agree with her assessment of the perceived problem or the new policy being considered. What active listening skills do you use with this officer?

SOLUTION

Give the officer the professional courtesy of finishing her thoughts without interrupting. Let occasional silences creep into your conversation. Allow a breath or

CASE STUDY 6, CONTINUED

two to occur within your conversation to show self-control and restraint and give the officer the time needed to create new thoughts without you jumping in to defend your position.

Make it a point to listen with your eyes and ears. Blink slowly. Because you're attentive, you see the officer giving subtle messages with body movements, eyes, and hand gestures. Be calm and attentive and watch for any clues that are being given every moment the officer is speaking to you.

Make a conscious choice not to judge the officer and remain silent while she is talking. You may not know where she is going with her thoughts, but give her a chance to speak openly without thinking to yourself, "She doesn't know what she's talking about." Be patient. Listen carefully and expect to get the information you'll need to respond with the right answer.

ISSUE

After this senior-ranking officer has finished telling you about the perceived problem and proposed a solution, how do you respond?

SOLUTION

Purposefully use short-sentence responses. Make positive and informed comments such as, "Yes, our IT department made us aware of that," or "We've been working to resolve that with the documentation department." Ask brief, pertinent questions to gather more information; this is a sign of respect and shows the officer you are listening. Repeat key points to the officer to let her know she's been heard. For example, "What you're saying is, the reason there is a need for this policy change is that a number of invoices were sent to old addresses. Is that right?" Then you stop and allow the officer to give her response. Repeating the officer's exact same language helps take the wind out of her sail because you've made a connection with her. You've maintained a level of professionalism despite your differing stances on the issue.

CASE STUDY 6, CONTINUED

Stick to discussing the policy change instead of changing the subject or defending your position on why the policy should or should not be changed. You stay connected. Changing the subject midstream breaks rapport and creates agitation, and the officer will leave feeling unheard and frustrated. The officer may not know the source of frustration but will be sure that you are not liked.

Control yourself. You may believe the officer is saying things that are incorrect, off-base, biased, uninformed, narrow-minded, and wrong, but you don't try to straighten the speaker out and set the record straight for the good of your department. If the officer becomes upset or accusatory, continue to listen carefully, remain in control of your emotions, and limit your reactions by responding in a way that is not inflammatory or aggressive. Remain calm no matter what transpires.

ISSUE

How do you follow up this discussion?

SOLUTION

Demonstrate respect and deference to the officer by asking if you should respond now or make an appointment to talk later so you can further evaluate the issues and develop a solution. Asking when the officer would like to receive your answer to their comments demonstrates respect. If you respond now, do so without defending yourself. State the facts as you know them and be brief in your comments.

CHAPTER SUMMARY

★ When other people are talking, you're in control of the conversation.

★ When practicing being a good listener, do not interrupt or ask questions. Stick to the topic, control yourself, blink slowly, and lean forward. Don't judge the speaker, remain calm, and listen with your eyes and ears.

★ When responding, use short sentences, allow for pauses, repeat what the speaker has said, stick to the topic, and use positive and informed language.

Communication Skills

ERE IS THE SECRET FOR BECOMING A great communicator: *Focus on giving people information the way they like to receive it, and they'll trust and listen to you with rapt attention.* If you give people information the way you like to, you'll lose your audience a great deal of the time. To communicate a thought, feeling, or idea to another person, it's best to mirror that person's communication style.

Salespeople spend their entire lives refining their personal rapport skills in order to gain a prospective customer's quick confidence and make a sale. On the opposite end of the spectrum, miscommunication and suspicious positions damage egos, maims careers, and costs

Definition of diplomacy: "Skill in handling affairs without arousing hostility."

Definition of a diplomat: "One who is employed or skilled at diplomacy."

—*Merriam Webster's Collegiate Dictionary,* 10th edition

businesses untold billions each year in internal and external *faux pas* and mistakes.

Benefits of Effective Communication

* Reduce fear
* Create income
* Make friends
* Become productive
* Experience less stress
* Avoid misunderstandings
* Create job satisfaction
* Improve your social life
* Enlarge your sphere of influence

The Four Channels of Basic Communication

> "You can make more friends in two months by becoming interested in other people than you can in two years by trying to get other people interested in you."
>
> —DALE CARNEGIE, MOTIVATIONAL SPEAKER AND AUTHOR, 1888–1955

The response you receive from your communication is a direct result of what the *other person understood you to say*. What the other person heard may or may not have anything to do with what you wanted to communicate. If you don't receive the desired response, change the way you're communicating.

Becoming flexible in your style of communication gives you a greater chance of getting what you want and reaping the best rewards. Effective communication is based on knowing what channel other people are using and speaking to them on it. You can learn what channel they're using by following this simple formula: Focus on the person with whom you're speaking and then speak his or her language.

The response you receive from your communication
is a direct result of what the other person
understood you to say.

Most people have an unconscious preference for using one channel of communication over another to speak and understand information they receive. The following are four different types of communicators.

1. *Visual.* Sixty percent of all people are motivated by sight. They hear by *visualizing* pictures. For example, they might say, "I *see* what you mean."

2. *Kinesthetic.* Twenty-five percent of all people are motivated by feeling. They *emotionally* interpret what they hear. For example, "I *feel* this is the right answer."

3. *Auditory.* Ten percent of all people are motivated by sound. They *listen* and process by hearing tone and inflection. For example, "I *hear* what you're saying."

4. *Auditory digital.* Five percent of all people are motivated by *information.* For example, "That's a *rational* answer."

If you focus on the way other people interpret the information you give and speak to them on the channel of communication they understand, they will (unconsciously) trust, like, and enjoy talking to you. Listen and watch carefully, and people will tell you how they process information so you can speak in a language they enjoy.

Knowing your own primary processing channel is NOT important. It is only important for you to know how to give people information on their favorite channel.

Ask a person to describe their office, and they will go inside for a moment and process the answer to your question in their own internal language. A visual person might use visually descriptive words. For example, "It has lots of sunlight and dark wood. The colors in my office are pale gray and white." An auditory person might use words that describe sound. For example, "It's noisy. We're on the first floor and we get sounds of traffic."

A kinesthetic person might use feeling words. For example, "It feels like a cocoon. I've got a really comfortable office." An auditory digital person might give you detailed information. For example, "We're in the Bank and Buffer Building on 11th Street and I'm on the 11th floor in suite 111."

The Visual Communicators

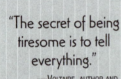

"The secret of being tiresome is to tell everything."

—Voltaire, author and philosopher, 1694–1778

Visual people enjoy seeing pictures in their mind's eye. Since 60 percent of all communicators are predominately visual, it makes sense to use words that paint pictures when you speak.

People who use the phrases such as, "I *looked* over the projections for this project," or "I *see* finishing this project by Friday" are generally visual communicators. They may also use many of the following visually descriptive words: look, show, glance, clear, notice, picture, image, sight, reveal, vision, and dull. Visual people speak at a faster pace than average; this is a great tip-off. They also enjoy action and fun, like bright colors, and dress stylishly. They don't actually hear much of what you're saying, so don't count on them to remember much. They're busy watching you and like to be shown how to do things. They are often perfectionists, and you're most likely to find them among salespeople, painters, photographers, architects, designers, artists, politicians, and others who consider themselves visually appreciative of beauty, color, shape, and design.

The Kinesthetic Communicators

Kinesthetic communicators relate deeply to their feelings and recognize and enjoy their emotional life. To keep the 25 percent of communicators who are kinesthetic people listening, you'll need to use words that closely relate to their feelings.

People who use the phrases such as, "I really *feel* we should do it this way," feel things deeply, and that's how they enjoy receiving information. Kinesthetic communicators also use words that describe feelings such as love, hate, warm, crushed, shocking, sad, and anxious. They understand and respond to feelings. They trust and enjoy experiencing their feelings. By giving them too much visual information, you risk breaking your connection with them because they will think you are superficial. Kinesthetic communicators are patient people who are caring and listen well. They speak much slower than visual communicators. Visual, auditory, and auditory digital communicators tend to find kinesthetics tedious and invasive. Kinesthetics appreciate comfort and ambience (sensible shoes, comfortable furniture, romantic movies), pleasure, holidays, intimate dinner parties, and cozy rooms. They also want people around them to be comfortable. They often are poets, musicians, actors and actresses, deeply religious or spiritual people, writers, community activists, gardeners, cooks, and others who acknowledge and live much of their lives in their feelings.

The Auditory Communicators

The auditory communicators deliver information with no translation into visual pictures or feelings. About 10 percent of all people listen to life.

People who use the phrases such as, "I *hear* what you're saying," or "It *sounds* good to me," process information only in words, without visual or kinesthetic language, so they prefer verbal feedback over written feedback. The majority of auditory communicators do not work well with visual communicators, and so they usually avoid them. Auditory communicators tend to find visual people extremely tedious and boring.

Auditory communicators use words such as communicate, say, tell, discuss, talk, silent, quiet, loud, shrill, audible, communicate, and loud. They like using the telephone, yet they are sensitive to external noises in an office or restaurant and are careful about the tone and volume they use in conversations, as well as being sensitive to other people's tone and volume. Auditory people may include singers, musicians, piano tuners, and others in the music business, incoming-call representatives, counselors, and therapists.

The Auditory Digital Communicators

A few people (less than 5 percent) communicate in a style called "auditory digital"; that is a nonfeeling, nonvisual language of science. Auditory digital communicators make comments such as, "I *understand*, and this is the answer." These communicators have the highest IQ scores of all the groups.

Those who communicate on the auditory digital channel have strong personalities and iron wills. They're often stubborn and opinionated. They enjoy receiving information in the form of data such as written reports, charts, and graphs so they can form their own opinion. They use words such as understand, objective, goal, effective, useful, analyze, relevant, compute, example, and manage. Auditory digital communicators appear to be unemotional and robotic but make a valuable contribution to the world as scientists, engineers, and accountants.

Most people are a combination of all four of these communication styles. The most common group consists of people who are visual and kinesthetic in varying or equal degrees.

CASE STUDY 7

Channels of Communication

ISSUE

A woman approaches you. You ask where she works, and she says, "I've worked for the JKL Company in Elm City for 14 years." What is her communication style?

SOLUTION

She is an auditory digital since she gave you *factual information*.

CASE STUDY 7, CONTINUED

ISSUE

How can you respond to the auditory digital woman in the example above?

SOLUTION

You speak to her in auditory digital language such as, "I understand that JKL Company has met many of their *objectives* this year."

ISSUE

A man says to you, "This has been such an exciting year for me. I'm really proud of my company." What is his communication style?

SOLUTION

He tells you he *feels* two things, excitement and pride, so you know he is kinesthetic.

ISSUE

How do you respond to this kinesthetic communicator?

SOLUTION

You say something such as, "The consumer *loves* your product. Your company is really *in touch* with your market."

ISSUE

You're standing in line at a buffet table at a business conference, next to you is a man who says, "Isn't this a terrific spread they've put out? Look at this ice sculpture of a huge fish surrounded by piles of pink shrimp." What is his communication style?

SOLUTION

He is a visual communicator.

ISSUE

How do you respond to this visual communicator?

SOLUTION

How about, "Did you see the fruit bar? *Red* strawberries and *blue*berries in the shape of a flag with *green* kiwis as the *stars*!"

CASE STUDY 7, CONTINUED

ISSUE

You're attending a conference in the auditorium of a banquet hall. When the speaker takes the stage, a woman next to you murmurs, "This is such a loud and boisterous group!" What is her communication style?

SOLUTION

She is an auditory communicator.

ISSUE

How can you respond to this auditory communicator?

SOLUTION

You might say, "The MC will *announce* that the room should *quiet* down and then they will *turn up* the *volume* on the speakers so we can *hear clearly*."

For more information about communication tools, refer to the reading list in the back of this book. The more you know about these tools, the better communicator you will be. There is no limit to the level of refinement you can develop by polishing, rehearsing, and experimenting with various communication tools. Remember, flexibility is a key factor in effective communication. Pay attention and mirror the styles of those speaking to you, and they will trust you instantly.

|||||||||||||||||||||||||||||||||||||

CHAPTER SUMMARY

★ The four styles of communication are visual, kinesthetic, auditory, and auditory digital.

★ People respond based on what they hear you say through their own style of communication.

Discussion and Décor

PEOPLE WANT TO HAVE ONLY ENOUGH information about you to evaluate your character when dealing with you in business. Most don't have the time or inclination during the average workday to get to know the *real you* and don't care about your pre-
vious life experiences or future plans and dreams. They want
to conduct business within the parameters of a polite (yet low-
impact) interaction without becoming entangled in your personal life.

There is a consistent hum of successful and unsuccessful
attempts at cordiality that enters into every business transac-
tion, telephone conversation, and daily encounter. After all,
how do you reveal your character in business without getting
too personal? What do you talk about if not talking about

business? Small talk in a business arena is a skill that is easily mastered by learning a simple technique called The 30-Day Rule.

The 30-Day Rule

The 30-Day Rule involves sharing impersonal information related to events that have occurred or will occur in your personal life during a 30-day span on either side of today.

Examples of the 30-Day Rule

- You're taking a bike trip in three weeks. Or, you took a bike trip last weekend.
- You're taking a class in two weeks. Or, you just took a class this weekend.
- You're buying a new car in three weeks. Or, you just bought a new car three weeks ago.
- You're planting a garden this weekend. Or, you planted a garden three weeks ago.
- You're painting the kitchen next Sunday. Or, you just painted the kitchen last Sunday.

Now that you have a basic understanding of the rules for making small talk in business, here are some guidelines to follow when you're having a business meal with people from your company or another one.

✔ Checklist: Making Small Talk in Business Dining Situations

- ❑ *Breakfast.* Make small talk until everyone has been handed their coffee; only then should you begin talking about business. If no one orders coffee, wait until breakfast has been ordered before talking about business.
- ❑ *Lunch.* Make small talk until everyone has ordered their lunch; then you can begin talking about business.
- ❑ *Dinner.* Make small talk for a minimum of 30 minutes before you begin talking about business.

✔ Checklist: Making Small Talk in Business Settings

Your rule for yourself is to practice the 30-Day Rule, but you may ask other people questions about themselves or their business to get information you need to conduct your business. If you're diplomatic, people will give you a surprising amount of information.

❑ *When you arrive at a meeting,* try to spend two or three minutes making small talk to develop a rapport with others.

❑ It's also good to spend two or three minutes *after a meeting* making small talk.

❑ Although small talk is common *during breaks in business meetings,* be aware that this is also a time for serious business conversations.

❑ *During social time* with business people, your job is to gather information from them; guard against offering too much about yourself by staying within the 30-Day Rule.

❑ Answer questions with professional directness. However, if you are *at a company function* (party, picnic, business conference) and are asked a probing and personal question you don't want to answer, consider applying The 30-Day Rule to keep from spilling too much personal information. Always remain professional and in control of your comments. You can respond to personal questions by sharing impersonal information about an *event* that relates to the question.

Say someone asks you "How's your wife's job?" You might respond "Thank you for asking. She's on her way to Portland this weekend to attend a seminar." This reveals an event (her trip) related to your wife's job yet provides no personal information.

Here's another example. Say someone asks "Where are you going on your vacation?" You don't what to tell them where you're going, so you respond "I just sent away for travel brochures for Colorado and information about cruises to Mexico." You reveal your research but not your vacation destination.

Telephone Small Talk

Small talk is difficult on the telephone. The best way to create the essence of small talk is to use prompts intended to get the person on the other end of the line to talk about themselves. You'll develop more rapport by being complimentary or inquisitive on the phone than by talking about yourself. For example, you might say to someone "That was very helpful. How did you learn to access that information so quickly?"

Of course, if this person is your friend or acquaintance, you can always use the 30-Day Rule to ask them about a fact regarding his or her life. Focus on the other person by asking something like "What will you do this weekend?" or "How was your vacation last week?" or "Will you go to the conference next week?" Always concentrate on the other person when speaking on the phone and stay current within 30 days.

CASE STUDY 8

Small Talk and the 30-Day Rule

ISSUE

You've been invited to have dinner with the manager of your department. How do you apply the 30-Day Rule?

SOLUTION

You apply the 30-Day Rule by making small talk for at least 30 minutes at the beginning of the meal. Discuss your spouse's job promotion she received three weeks ago, a tennis tournament you're playing in next weekend with the company-sponsored league, and your purchase of new software for your home computer. You can always talk about the weather; it's a dull subject but a classic example of the 30-Day Rule since it's an impersonal current event.

ISSUE

Your manager asks, "What things are important to you outside of work?"

CASE STUDY 8, CONTINUED

SOLUTION

You respond by telling about something that reveals your inner values and shows your character in a positive light but offers information related to an event. For example, "I care about my family and community. My wife and I are involved in local community events. This Saturday we're Walking-for-Dollars to raise money for a back-to-school book-buying program in our neighborhood."

Decorating Your Personal Office Space

Self-expression is one of the hallmarks of the American way of life. When you decorate personal space in your office, make wise choices that reflect your professional persona, rank, and title.

While stuffed animals or dancing hula dolls in grass skirts are cute perched on top of your computer monitor, in many offices they're considered unprofessional. Remaining conservative in your décor is better than creating an office that gives people more information than they need about the real you. Although some industries encourage creative self-expression, it's still wise to display things that put your character in a favorable light. Try to avoid décor that might make people wonder about your level of sanity or honesty. It's far better to be thought of as dull than of questionable character.

> "Like the bee, we should make our industry our amusement."
> —OLIVER GOLDSMITH, ANGLO/IRISH POET AND DRAMATIST, 1728–1774

Suggestions for Decorating Your Office Space

Choose items for your office that reflect pertinent information you want your associates to know regarding your education, family, hobbies, and industry-related activities. Your office décor should be based on the image you'd like to project.

- Keep toys at home.
- Throw away dead or dying plants. Unless you have a green thumb and plants that will survive on little water

and sunlight, opt for a form of self-expression other than office foliage.

- Put pictures of your family in pleasing frames and hang on the walls or place them on your desk. Avoid taping photographs around your desk or on your computer monitor.
- Do not display greeting cards, outdated holiday decorations, food, or medication (prescription or over-the-counter). Put all these things away in cabinets so they cannot be seen.
- Keep any political posters out of sight.
- While you may love your children's art, don't hang it in your office unless it's framed.
- Keep religious art to a minimum in your office, even if you're a deeply religious person.
- The following make good office decorations: framed pictures of your family; one or two personal possessions such as diplomas, industry certifications, awards, and professional trophies; silk flower arrangements; industry-related books; and well-appointed office supplies such as a clean desk blotter, filing cabinets, chairs and table.

CASE STUDY 9

Personal Office Décor

ISSUE

You've just been promoted to the position of vice president in your company and are moving into a private office. What are some basic decorative items you could use?

SOLUTION

You might hang a framed college diploma along with any certificates or industry awards for excellence or a framed photo of your family. On the bookshelf, you might set a photo of a beloved pet or a sailboat you own along with a dozen books related to your industry. You could even put a bronze replica on your desk of the product your company makes. A clean blotter on your desk is also a nice touch.

‖‖‖‖‖‖‖‖‖‖‖‖‖‖‖‖‖‖‖‖‖‖‖‖‖

CHAPTER SUMMARY

★ The 30-Day Rule involves sharing impersonal information related to events that have occurred or will occur in your life during a span of 30 days on either side of today.

★ When making small talk on the telephone, use prompts intended to get the person on the other end of the line to talk about personal happenings.

★ When you decorate your personal space in your office, make wise choices that reflect your professional persona, your job description, and demeanor.

Professional Appearance

> "Every generation laughs at the old fashions, but follows religiously the new."
>
> —HENRY DAVID THOREAU, AMERICAN ESSAYIST AND POET, 1817–1862

I F YOU HAVE BRIGHT EYES, A GREAT SMILE, clear skin, and a healthy appearance, the world instinctively reacts to you in a positive way. It's a proven evolutionary fact that people respond to attractive, well-groomed, healthy, and energetic people more positively than they do to those who appear ungroomed, sickly, and lacking energy. Perhaps it's part of our primal instinct regarding survival of the fittest that makes people unconsciously gravitate to a healthy tribe for their basic survival needs.

As you learned in Chapter 6, 60 percent of people are visual communicators. That means that in 60 percent of the world, your image is important to the way other people perceive you, even if it's not important to you. The way you present yourself and the choices you make about colors, fabrics, style, and care of your clothing give clues to the people around you about your lifestyle, habits, attention to detail, sense of style, and even your belief systems. When other people look at you, they unconsciously assume they understand your priorities and attitudes about life. Your image also provides nonverbal clues to people about the way you see yourself and want the world to see you.

The Businesswoman

Tailored dressing is the key word for women in business. As a woman, you've got flexibility in your wardrobe choices; you can wear bright colors and a layered look or opt for subdued colors in a dress or pantsuit. Either way, make your wardrobe choices conducive to a business atmosphere and avoid baggy sweaters or pants. There's no doubt that looser fitting clothing are more comfortable, but they're looked upon as weekend attire and not acceptable for the office.

Ladies, while the glass ceiling may be cracked and in a few cases broken, women are still creating innovative ways to exercise their power and authority in the world and workplace. It hasn't been that many years since Rosie the Riveter flexed her right bicep in the famous World War II poster that stated in bold headlines, "We can do it. " In her red polka-dot Women's Ordnance Worker's bandana and coveralls, she extended an invitation to the women of her day to join her and step forward to serve the war effort. Today, women are walking into boardrooms wearing pantyhose and two-inch heels and still saying, "We can do it." Many of them are reaching their career goals instead of just hoping their daughters will have a broader range of opportunities.

A woman's image is important to her career development. In order to compete in today's job market, she must look vital and healthy and appear to have the energy required to be taken seriously in the daily commerce of business. The more professional you act, and the more polished and healthy you appear, the greater your chance of reaching your career goals. You don't need to dress or act like a man to succeed, but you do need to find ways to be perceived as a professional person to develop self-confidence and self-esteem in a business world still heavily dominated by men. Once you taste and understand that core feeling of "I can do it," you can recall that sense of power again and again as you make your way up the corporate ladder.

There are many ways to experience a sense of yourself as a professional woman. One of the best ways (aside from the application of talents and skills related to your job) is for you to feel and look good in your professional wardrobe. You don't need a closet filled with St. John Knits (although that would be a dream-come-true for many women), but you do need a few *quality items* that fit well and flatter your figure, coloring, and personality.

In many ways, men have a much easier time creating a working wardrobe for themselves. They have adopted a uniform approach to their business dress. If women adopted this approach and were willing to sacrifice some of their need for variety, it would be less expensive and less time-consuming, and they would have fewer problems with low self-esteem and competitiveness in the workplace. This is not to suggest that women sacrifice their style, flair, or color choices. It does mean, however, that owning fewer clothes of high quality is a better investment of money and time than having a closet full of poor-quality garments that don't last beyond a season. Classic clothes are a better choice than variety in your wardrobe any day. It makes more sense to purchase a $100 skirt that is lined and well-tailored and will last for years than four $25 skirts that are made of inferior fabric, unlined, poorly constructed, and won't last past a single season. Think of your wardrobe as an investment in your career rather than as an opportunity to make a daily fashion statement to the world.

This Woman Makes Sense

Every corporate culture and industry has its own dress code, ranging from formal dress to overalls. There are no one-size-fits-all answers for women regarding dressing in the workplace. Some companies allow employees to wear more casual clothes in summer months. The entertainment industry encourages sensual dress and makes pantyhose optional. Many sectors of technology allow jeans and tennis shoes.

Here are some suggestions from Sherry Maysonave, president and founder of Empowerment Enterprises. She is a nationally respected business image consultant and author of *Casual Power: How to Power Up Your Nonverbal Communication and Dress Down for Success.*[1] She makes a lot of sense for those of you who are dressing for corporate America.

What Does Business-Casual Mean for Women?

Business-casual is a comfortably relaxed version of traditional business attire that does not sacrifice professionalism or personal power. It's not sloppy casual or kicked-back weekend wear; it still has a tailored and businesslike look.

It's not as easy to describe business-casual dress for women as for men since women have so many more choices for creating the look. For example, business-casual dress for a client of mine who is a large woman is a long skirt, jacket, and a layered knit blouse. For other women, it may include a knee-length skirt with a twin sweater set, tailored jacket, and hose. For most women, business-casual includes pants.

Business-casual shoes are not sandals or opened toed shoes. They have a closed toe and heel. Beyond that, they are a matter of a woman's personal style and preference. She should wear a short heel (1-1½ inches) to elevate her height.

Women have to work harder than a man at being perceived as powerful and highly professional in a business environment. They need to *power up* their casualwear more in order to get ahead and be successful.

---

[1] Sherry Maysonave, information@casualpower.com.

What About the Care and Maintenance of Business-Casual Clothing?

Beware of cotton and linen as business-casual wear. They are both time-consuming and expensive to maintain. Cotton should be sent to the cleaners unless you love to iron. Although starch is an individual preference in the body of a garment, collars and cuffs should be starched since cotton needs to be crisp for it to hang correctly. The linen look has been called snobby wrinkles and is not well-suited for business wear unless you're in the fashion industry or you work in a resort. Nonverbally, linen says resort attire.

> The linen look has been called snobby wrinkles and is not well-suited for business wear unless you're in the fashion industry or you work in a resort. Nonverbally, linen says resort attire.

What Fabrics Are More Appropriate than Cotton and Linen?

Lightweight wool and silk-blends are better choices for business-casual. They do need to be dry-cleaned but not as often as cotton or linen, if taken care of regularly. A woman should send her 100 percent wool clothing to the dry cleaner every two or three months unless something is especially soiled. She should always check for spots after wearing wools. She can also have her wool clothes steamed instead of dry-cleaned.

What Are Some Examples of Good Care for Business-Casual Clothing?

When a woman gets home, she should hang her clothes up on the appropriate hangers in a closet that is not overcrowded. Clothes that are cramped in a closet need to be dry-cleaned more often than those allowed to breathe between wearings. Home steaming is also a great way to care for clothes. She can fill her bathtub with hot water, turn the tap off and hang the clothes in the hot steamy bathroom. That's an an inexpensive way to let the wrinkles fall out.

What About Khaki for a Business-Casual Look?

The fabric and color of khaki are not flattering to a woman's figure unless she's blonde and thin. Khaki is also hard to care for since it begins to shrink after several washings.

What About Wearing Sleeveless Garments as a Business-Casual Look?

Sleeveless dressing is considered social attire, and it diminishes workplace credibility. A woman may have beautiful arms, and she may look great in sleeveless blouses or tops, but this makes her less believable than if she were wearing sleeves or a jacket.

What Kinds of Accessories Are Appropriate for a Woman to Wear in a Work Environment?

A woman should consider wearing simple accessories that draw attention to her face such as earrings and necklaces. Necklaces that are too long or busy draw attention away from her face. It's worth investing in a good pair of earrings. While gold and platinum are at the top of the line, a casual metal such as sterling silver is fine. She should reserve her big scarves for social dressing; they can be hard to handle in the workplace and make many women look frumpy.

What Kinds of Watches Are Good for a Business Environment?

A woman should always leave her sports watch at home. Gold, silver, or stainless steel watchbands are more professional; leather straps are considered casual or social. The face of her watch should be slightly larger, too, since small-faced watches are considered social.

What Kind of Handbags Should Women Take to Work?

A woman should avoid anything that looks like a shopping bag. Shoulder-strap bags are best in the colors black, navy, or maybe brown. Big handles on a purse can make a woman look like she's a socialite headed out for lunch or shopping. She should carry as little as necessary; an organizer, a briefcase and a purse is too much.

How Many Outfits do Women Need to Appear Professional?

It's best for a woman to buy separates and to create more variety in her wardrobe so she can mix and match her clothes. She should have five casual outfits that include pants, blouses, jackets, and skirts; and three business suits that are not matching but coordinated separates. If she buys quality pieces and cares for them, she'll have enough to fit in most business environments.

What Kind of Outdoor Gear Does a Woman Need in a Business Environment?

A woman who lives in a cold climate needs an ankle-length topcoat that is preferably 100 percent wool. The ideal would be a cashmere coat in black, navy, or brown. Her raingear should be slightly fitted with a belt that reveals her basic silhouette.

Does Wearing Makeup Enhance a Woman's Professional Image?

Research has shown that women who tastefully apply their makeup have 20 percent to 30 percent higher incomes. The world likes to see a woman who appears polished and professional. Other studies show that women who wear too much makeup and those who don't wear any at all are both perceived as having low self-esteem. It's as if the woman who's wearing too much makeup is trying to hide and the one who wears no makeup at all is saying "Why try?"

Are There Certain Hairstyles that Are Appropriate for Work?

A woman's hair should suit her face shape, lifestyle, and personal style; however if it is longer than 2" below her shoulders, it should be pulled up or back. If she wants to look business-savvy, she shouldn't use banana clips to pull it back since these would make her look like she just walked out of the gym or bedroom. She shouldn't sport a swinging, teenage ponytail either.

Is Hair-Coloring Appropriate for the Business Environment?

A woman's hair color should not be garish or draw too much attention to the fact that it's obviously colored. Many of the trendy, frosted-hair highlights are too dramatic for the workplace. Again, women need to look dynamic and like they have the energy it takes to conduct business.

It's also important to be careful with home hair-color jobs since they can turn out looking uneven and defeat a woman's purpose of trying to look professional.

How Often Should a Woman Update Her Wardrobe?

A woman should address her wardrobe needs year-round to check for spots or missing buttons. She should consider buying clothes that are worn nine months of the year and not considered seasonal purchases when building her wardrobe. She can add or take out items twice a year during fall/winter and spring/summer. Spring/summer clothes are not as businesslike and long-lasting, but there are some great lightweight yet durable tropical wools and silks that are comfortable in warm climates.

What Are Power Colors for Women?

Power colors for women are solid ones. They include black, navy, red, purple, certain shades of green, yellow, rich reds, and dark grays. Women should stick to strong colors when they want to look powerful and shouldn't wear too many at the same time.

Where Do Women Get Ideas for Professional Dressing?

Hollywood. Women have always imitated what they see their favorite movie stars doing. They watch movies and television and copy what they see on the screen. It's not always right and doesn't always work for office dressing, but that's where many women get their fashion ideas.

The Businessman

Gentlemen, whether you organize and care for your own professional wardrobe or your spouse offers to help you accomplish this important aspect of your career, this chapter shows you how to create a powerful and attractive business image. You'll learn the secrets for quickly building and caring for a wardrobe with minimal investment.

The truth is, you don't need to invest in the most expensive or trendy fashions available each year. However, you do need to invest in a few well-tailored garments and then take the time to care for them.

The technology boom of the late 20th century spawned a culture of talented people who sported jeans, T-shirts, and tennis shoes at work seven days a week. Many of those in the technology sector owned only one suit or sport jacket that hung in the back of their closets for weddings, funerals, and board meetings.

As long as these technology programmers did their jobs, their employers allowed them to dress as comfortably as they wanted to dress while working in their offices. A human resource manager for one of the big high-tech companies in San Francisco once joked, "No, we don't have a dress code here. In fact, at our company, shoes are optional." But we can't all be high-tech dressers, nor should we want to be. Your clothing tells people who you are.

Men's Apparel Questions Answered

"Stand tall and dress well and expect to prosper."

—MESSAGE FOUND IN A FORTUNE COOKIE IN CHICAGO, ILLINOIS

Rodney Cole, corporate accounts manager for the popular chain of men's clothing stores, *Men's Wearhouse* [2], is a prominent image consultant for today's professional male. He travels extensively and teaches today's contemporary businessmen the guidelines for creating a professional business image. Here, Cole answers important questions about creating a man's professional image in today's business world.

While Technology Companies Have Enjoyed Two Decades of a More Relaxed Work Environment, Do You Think the Rest of American Business Has Relaxed Dress Codes for Their Employees?

Yes, in business today, eight out of ten companies use the business-casual Friday dress code all five days of the week. However, in most of those companies, senior-level executives still wear a sport coat with a tie, or a suit and tie five days a week.

What Is Business-Casual?

What it's *not* is cotton twill pants and a golf shirt with tennis shoes. But it is a pair of nice wool-gabardine slacks with a heavy-gauge

---

[2] Rodney Cole, Men's Wearhouse, (800) 777-8580, extension 8701, recole1@charter.net.

cotton polo shirt or mock turtleneck and a sport coat. If a man wears a sport coat, his look is business-casual. Without a sport coat, it's casual.

How Many Pairs of Wool-Gabardine Slacks Should a Man Have? What Colors Should They Be?

A man needs to know that the more clothes he has in his wardrobe, the less wear they'll get and the longer they will last. Secondly, the better care he takes of his wardrobe, the longer it will last. To create a nice slacks wardrobe, a man should own a minimum of five pairs in black, navy, medium gray, charcoal, and an earth tone (taupe or olive gray). He should have the pants dry-cleaned every four or five wearings. If they are the only slacks he owns, he'll wear each pair once a week or an average of 48 times per year. You can see how hard that would be on a wardrobe with fewer than five pairs of slacks.

How Many Mock Turtlenecks Should a Man Have for Business-Casual Dress?

Mock turtlenecks are a great way for a man to feel dressed up without looking dressy. It's a way of cheating. To be on the safe side, a man should have at least five mock turtlenecks in his wardrobe. Remember, the more clothes he has, the longer they will last before needing replacing.

How Many Polo Shirts Should a Man Have in His Business-Casual Wardrobe?

A polo shirt has two to four buttons on the front. It has short sleeves and looks like a golf shirt. Polo shirts come in a wide variety of colors. They should be sent to the dry cleaners so they'll keep their shape for the business-casual look. This will also help the colors and fibers last longer than if the shirts are thrown in the washer and dryer. A man should have a minimum of five polo shirts in his business-casual wardrobe.

Should a Man Wear an Undershirt or T-Shirt under his Mock Turtleneck, Polo Shirt, or Dress Shirt?

Generally, if a man's father wore T-shirts, he will wear them. It depends on how you were taught. If a man is particularly hairy, it's important for him to wear a T-shirt under a light-colored shirt for cosmetic reasons. T-shirts are also good if a man perspires a lot.

How Many Sport Coats Should a Man Own? What Kind Should They Be?

A man should own five sport coats: two blazers and three fancy ones. A fancy sport coat is one that has a checked, plaid, or geometric design.

What Are the Other Differences Between a Blazer and a Sport Coat?

A blazer is timeless, and every man should have both a black and a navy one with brass, gold, or silver buttons in his business-casual wardrobe. A sport coat has bone buttons just like the ones on a suit. Two or three buttons on a sport coat are classic and traditional. Coats with four or five buttons are trendy and fashion-forward but generally go out of style in a few seasons.

What Colors Do You Recommend for Sport Coats in a Business-Casual Wardrobe?

A man should get a sport coat in gray, navy, or earth tones (olive, taupe, or tans).

How Should a Sport Coat Fit a Man?

The sport coat should be large enough in the shoulders to extend past the shoulder line a little bit. It should have a deep armhole so it doesn't pull up and bind the man under the arm. He should be able to button the coat and then pull it out in front and drop a grapefruit down the opening. The sleeves should never extend past the wrist and break into the palm. Women's jackets do break slightly into the palm, but men's do not.

Are There Shoes You'd Consider Business-Casual?

Casual shoes for business are slip-on and always in leather. The lightweight shoe is fashionable but hard on the foot and doesn't offer much support. A substantial shoe is more comfortable as long as the sole of the shoe is not too thick and doesn't look like fat rubber. Lace-up shoes are also OK for business-casual, and a man should always wear them with suits.

What Are the Choice Colors for Business-Casual Shoes?

Black and cordovan (burgundy) or cognac-colored shoes are great choices for a man.

What About the Care of Shoes?

Business shoes are a big investment in a man's wardrobe, and he should take care of them so they'll last a long time. Leather shoes should be paste-polished and buffed often, and he should put liquid edge dressing on the edge of the soles to keep them looking clean. The liquid edge dressing also protects the shoe to a certain extent. The most important thing he needs to do is put cedar shoe trees in his shoes when he's not wearing them. Good shoes wear from the inside out. Most men perspire a couple of ounces of moisture a day, and that perspiration draws back the leather when the shoe is not being worn and ruins the shape of the shoe. The cedar in a shoe tree absorbs the moisture, keeps the shoe straight, and helps extend the life of his shoes by 30 to 40 percent.

What About Socks?

There's only one sock that is appropriate, but most men hate it. It comes up over the calf and ends just under the knee. Most men wear ankle or medium-length socks, even though they're always pulling them up throughout the day. A man will get used to higher socks quickly if he'll try them, since he'll never have to touch them during the day. When a man crosses his leg in public to take tension off his knee, he shouldn't let the skin show between his sock and pant leg. High socks are cosmetic as well as functional.

How Are Sock Colors Chosen? Is There a Rule to Follow?

A man should try to match his socks to the color of his trousers or slacks. In other words, wear black socks with black pants, navy with navy, olive with olive, and tan with tan. Granted, he'll never match his socks and slacks perfectly, but he should try to come as close as possible.

How Many Suits and Shirts Should a Man Have in His Wardrobe? What Colors Should He Have?

A man should own five business suits. The most popular colors are solid navy, solid charcoal, navy stripe, gray stripe, and earth tone (olive, taupe or tan in summer). He should wear a nice pinpoint oxford shirt with his suit. An executive needs to own a minimum of two week's worth of garments or ten full outfits. This means he'll wear each of his suits 24 times a year. It's good to rotate one of those suits out of his inventory each year and replace it with a new one.

Will You Speak to the Issue of Dress Shirts with Suits?

A man should buy and wear only cotton shirts. Yes, it's $5 to $15 more per shirt, but it looks better, it's dressier, and the cotton shirt lasts longer. A light starch gives it body and crispness. There are three kinds of dress shirts: button-down, plain collar (also called point or spread collar), and tab collar. The only two shirts to wear with a suit are plain collar and tab collar. The plain collar has no buttons to secure the shirt body to the collar. The button down should be worn with sport coats but not with suits. White shirts are predominately worn in business, but men can wear muted colors like pale blue, cream, or ecru; French blue (a darker, vivid blue) is also popular.

Why Are Lace-Up Shoes More Appropriate with Suits?

Lace-up shoes are the only thing a man should wear with suits. The most popular dress shoe sold over the last six decades is called a captoe shoe. He should have one black and one burgundy pair.

Are There Any Rules for Ties?

There are three rules for ties that a man should follow. First, he should only wear silk ties with suits. He can wear cotton or wool ties with sport coats or under sweaters for a casual look. Second, the smaller the knot the better. Third, his tie should hang between the top of his waistband and two inches below his waist.

What About Wearing Pocket Silks in the Breast Pocket of His Suit?

A pocket silk or linen pocket square is always a great look with a suit. It should stick out of a man's breast pocket about half an inch. He can wear either a white one all the time or match the silk to an accent color in his tie. It can either be squared (this is most common) or folded in a variety of other ways. The important thing is that it not hang outside the pocket. It's meant to be a suggestion of color.

Do You Have Any Advice for Men About their Nails and Hair?

A man's fingernails should always be clean, short, and groomed. Some men look great in long hair, but most do not. A man should wear his hair short and have a traditional cut that is blocked in back; this is considered professional. Facial hair should be kept trimmed daily.

What About Accessories such as Jewelry?

A few good pieces of jewelry are enough. An elegant watch (not a sports watch) is a great accessory. Necklaces and heavy bracelets are not appropriate for business dress.

What About Rain and Cold Weather Gear?

A trench coat is meant to repel but not stop water completely during a rainstorm. Trench coats generally have a lining that zips out for spring and summer. A topcoat is dressier and more professional looking and is worn in colder climates. A good-looking choice would be a cashmere-wool blend, or camel hair, and it can be worn either in a double or single-breasted style.

How Often Should a Man Update His Wardrobe?

Twice a year is great. That may seem too often, but it's a good idea for a man to check his closet at least twice a year to make sure he has what he wants and needs to look and feel like a professional businessman.

CHAPTER SUMMARY

Women's Appearance

Business-casual is a comfortably relaxed version of traditional business attire that doesn't sacrifice professionalism or personal power.

★ Women need to power up their casual wear more than men do to get ahead and be successful.

★ Lightweight wools or silk blends are a better choice for business-casual than cotton or linen.

★ Women should own a good pair of earrings and a watch with a larger face and a metal band.

★ It's a great idea to carry a shoulder strap bag in black, navy, or brown.

★ A woman needs five full casual outfits and three full business suits.

★ A woman should wear a moderate amount of well-applied makeup and her hair above the shoulders or pulled back or off her face. Avoid wearing garish or obvious hair coloring.

★ Women's power colors are black, navy, red, purple, and certain shades of green, yellow, olive, rich red, and dark gray.

Men's Appearance

★ Business-casual is defined by wearing a pair of nice wool-gabardine pants with a heavy-gauge golf shirt or mock turtleneck. A sport coat is also worn.

★ A man needs a minimum of five pairs of wool-gabardine slacks in his wardrobe.

★ A man needs five polo shirts and five mock turtlenecks.

★ A man needs five sport coats, including two blazers (one black and one navy with brass, gold, or silver buttons) and three fancy sport coats (with a pattern, checked, plaid, or geometric design). The three fancy sport coats should be in gray, navy, or earth tones (olive or taupe).

★ Slip-on or lace shoes can be worn with sport coats. Only lace shoes should be worn with a suit. Business-casual and lace-up shoes are black, cordovan (burgundy), or cognac in color. Cedar shoe trees should always be used.

★ Knee socks are preferable to short ankle socks.

★ A businessman needs to own five business suits. He needs two weeks' worth of garments or ten full outfits.

★ A man should wear only cotton shirts. Button-down shirts are worn with sport coats. Plain collar shirts are worn with suits.

★ Silk ties are worn with suits. Cotton or wool ties are worn with sport coats.

Getting the Job

H AVING GREAT SKILLS AND IMPECCABLE references doesn't necessarily mean you'll get the job you're after. Why not? Because if the person interviewing you doesn't think you'll be a *fit* for the position (regardless of the reason), you won't be considered for it.

Today's employers are searching for skilled and talented people who will fit into their company's structure and become dedicated partners in its growth efforts over a long period of time. Knowing this important criterion should prepare you to walk into a job interview and convince a potential employer that you can fit into the company, have the necessary skills for the job, and want a career in that firm.

Chemistry is an important component during a job interview. If you and your interviewer don't click and make a positive connection, you won't get past your initial interview, nor will you get the job since you don't seem to be a fit. This may sound unprofessional or even harsh, but if you want a particular job and you believe you are totally qualified, it's also your task to create positive chemistry with the interviewer as you discuss your skills and work history.

You must be personable during your interview and present yourself as someone with likeable qualities as well as a skilled and qualified candidate for the job.

There is a set of skills to use during an interview that will give you the self-confidence you'll need when sitting across a desk from a human resource manager or recruiter. If you think you're there only to find out about the job opening, you're missing an enormous chance to establish positive chemistry with your interviewer. It's important for you to show that you're interested in the company as well as the job.

It's important for you to show your interviewer that
you're interested in the company
as well as the job.

Fran Pomerantz[1] specializes in executive search for the digital media (Internet and video-on-demand). She tells her clients to be patient. "In today's economy, it often takes companies between two months and a year to make a decision before hiring. Because interviews are so important, it's normal to be

---

[1] Fran Pomerantz, The Pomerantz Group, (310) 319-6100, fpomerantz@ pomerantzgroup.com, 2001 Wilshire Blvd., #400, Santa Monica, CA 90403, www.pomerantzgroup.com.

nervous during the interview and talk instead of listen. It's critical to listen and answer questions carefully instead of just asking, trying to get information from the interviewer about the position that's open. There will come a time when you can (and should) ask about the company during the interview, but be patient."

Scenario Setup: Your Job Interview

➤ Your interview begins the moment you have your first contact on the telephone with anyone from your prospective company. Be pleasant and enthusiastic and listen more than you talk.

➤ Don't volunteer information unless you're asked for it.

➤ Prior to your interview, get a haircut if necessary, check the clothing you plan to wear, polish and edge your shoes, and clip and manicure your nails.

➤ Get enough rest the night before.

➤ When you greet your interviewer, stand, offer a warm and sincere handshake, smile, give a one or two-second eyebrow flash, introduce yourself, and immediately thank the person for his or her time.

➤ Since you'll be shaking your interviewer's hand with your right hand, you should have your (flat, unfolded) resume in your left hand in a large, 9-by-12-inch envelope to protect it from being creased, smudged, or wrinkled. Hold on to it until the interviewer asks for it.

➤ Follow the interviewer to the private office that has been arranged for your interview. When you reach that office, ask where you should sit and then take your seat.

➤ Make a second rapport-building comment to your interviewer to indicate you are professional and relaxed. It's always safe to compliment the company's facility, such as saying "This is a nice office." You could also comment about the location of the facility, "This is an ideal location. It's convenient to the freeway."

➤ As the interviewer takes your resume from you and removes it from the envelope, appear relaxed and don't stare the person down as she or he reads it. Allow your eyes to wander several feet on either side of the interviewer. Don't swing your head around and look at the office.

➤ When the interview begins, maintain good eye contact with your interviewer but don't forget to blink. It's fine to glance away occasionally to keep the interviewer from feeling self-conscious about being stared down.

➤ Allow the interviewer to set the pace. Don't take control of the interview; wait for your cue to ask any questions you'd like answered.

➤ Once the questions begin, keep your hands in your lap and do not let them fly about the air like birds out of their cage. They should be completely still unless you're using them to make a specific point.

➤ If you do want to make a pertinent point, it's OK to use one or both hands for emphasis. Place the fingertips of one hand on the interviewer's desk as you say, "That project taught me the importance of being a part of a team." Placing your entire opened hand on the table assumes ownership and can be construed as aggressive. If there is no table, create an invisible one in front of you and place one hand on it to make your point. It's a bit theatrical, but a powerful gesture to make.

➤ You may also use both hands to make an occasional gesture but avoid pointing, scratching anywhere on your body, or touching any part of your face or head.

➤ Appear alert and enthusiastic during your initial interview. Don't become too relaxed. Do this by sitting with your buttocks in the middle of the chair or closer to the edge of the chair. Be careful to check yourself for correct posture since it's tempting to slump after a few minutes. Practice sitting in the middle or on the edge of your chair at home before trying it during the interview.

➢ Remember to smile occasionally while you are speaking. It's easy to forget to smile during an interview because of nervousness, so allow yourself to do it while talking. It's a good way to show self-confidence.

➢ Answer the interviewer's questions with relatively short responses. Avoid rambling and stay on the subject.

➢ Regardless of how unhappy or unsatisfied you were with your former company (or boss), find positive things to say. Ranting on about what a miserable place it was to work will create a bad impression with your interviewer, even if your rants are true.

➢ When your interviewer asks if you have any questions, appear enthusiastic about the opportunity to learn the answers to a few questions about the company or the possibilities for advancement.

➢ As the interview winds down, thank the interviewer for his or her time. When the interviewer stands or gives you signals that the time is up, that's your cue to stand.

➢ Offer to shake your interviewer's hand and thank her or him again on your way out the door for the opportunity to apply for the job and for giving you information about the company.

➢ Send an e-mail or handwritten thank-you note as soon as possible thanking the interviewer once again for his or her time and the opportunity to apply for the job within the company.

Leesa McElroy's Interview Tips

Leesa McElroy, the staffing manager of a Fortune 500 international retailer, annually interviews more than 1,000 people who are looking for new jobs. She calls her company a traditional one with conservative values and believes people should understand the process when interviewing for a job with her company. The following are her nine suggestions for your interview.

> "Forty percent of new employees hired by management fail in their first jobs. The key reason for this failure is their inability to build good relationships with peers and subordinates."
> —STUDY BY MANCHESTER PARTNERS INTERNATIONAL, 1997

1. Be on time. No, *be early*. "Early is on time, and on time is late." So often, recent graduates haven't yet learned the value of time and are not punctual.

2. Show up early for your interview so you can fill out your job application.

||||||||||||||||||||||||||||||||||||||||||||||||||||||||||||||||||||||||||||||||||||||||||||||||||||||||||||||||||||||||||||||||||

No interviewer likes to hear, "I don't have all the information with me."

||||||||||||||||||||||||||||||||||||||||||||||||||||||||||||||||||||||||||||||||||||||||||||||||||||||||||||||||||||||||||||||||||

3. Come prepared with any telephone numbers and work history dates you may need to fill out your application properly. No interviewer likes to hear, "I don't have all the information with me."

4. It's important to ask questions about the company. Otherwise, it looks as though you haven't done your homework and don't know enough about the company to ask questions.

5. Dress a full notch above what you think is expected of you. For instance, if you're a man applying for a job in a company that practices business-casual dress on Fridays (or all week), you should still wear a suit and tie or a sport coat and tie. A woman should wear pantyhose and closed-toe shoes and leave her sandals at home in the closet. Pants are OK, but a skirt is more appropriate.

6. A recent graduate should have a one-page resume. A person with some work history should have a two-page resume. It can be single-spaced with a double space between job listings.

7. Allow enough time for your interview. A phone-screen interview lasts about 20 to 30 minutes, but when you come to an office, you need to come early enough to fill out your application. Allow plenty of time and don't be rushed during a face-to-face interview.

8. Appear enthusiastic. Don't be afraid to show enthusiasm for the company and the job.

9. Remain professional. Don't make the mistake of becoming too familiar with your interviewer. Avoid giving personal answers instead of professional ones. It's a mistake for you to think you've gotten the job and begin to assume that it is yours. Do everything you can to keep a high tone and remain completely professional.

Your Resume

To create a professional resume, look for free templates on the Internet or invest in affordable software available in most office supply stores. These templates will enable you to tailor your resume to highlight your skills for each of your job interviews. For more information about vital interview skills, refer to the reading list in the back of this book.

CHAPTER SUMMARY

★ If you fail to create positive chemistry during a job interview, you won't get the job.

★ Be early for your interview to fill out your application.

★ Dress a notch above what is expected of you for a job interview.

★ Ask questions about the company during your interview. Show enthusiasm.

★ Write a thank-you note or send an e-mail thank-you message to your interviewer.

Rising
in the
Corporation

CHAPTER

10

Moving Up the Corporate Ladder

> "Big shots are only little shots who keep shooting."
> —CHRISTOPHER MORLEY,
> AMERICAN EDITOR AND WRITER,
> 1890–1957

NTERNAL NETWORKING MAY SOUND LIKE A strange concept. However, on closer examination, you'll see that not knowing the profile and personalities of key leaders in your company will put you at an extreme disadvantage since you won't understand the people at the top of the chain of command.

Once you examine the process for internal networking, you'll quickly see that the rewards for your efforts far outweigh any inconvenience or reluctance you might initially experience. Ignore the issues surrounding internal networking, and you risk being passed up and becoming a part of corporate obscurity (shudder at the thought).

Most companies like to seek out employees within their ranks to groom as future leaders of their organization.

Senior-level managers want to educate future leaders for the task of carrying on with their ultimate corporate missions. You may be perfectly suited for promotion in your company, but if senior management doesn't recognize your strengths and know who you are because you've avoided drawing too much attention to yourself, you could easily be passed up for advancement.

It's clear that your career is your total responsibility to manage and plan. Don't wait for a Hollywood plot twist in hopes you'll be discovered and promoted because of a flashing stroke of luck. Begin acting in a way that reflects your talents and enthusiasm and expect doors to open for you that otherwise would not have existed. Many progressive companies identify and groom their future talent, but other companies do not. You stand a far greater chance of climbing the corporate ladder by finding ways to promote yourself internally than by waiting for the ideal circumstances to reveal themselves and make you into a rising star.

Creating Your Game Plan

> "Plans are nothing; planning is everything."
> —Dwight D. Eisenhower, 34th President of the United States, 1890–1969

You can strike gold by having a keen curiosity and being willing to do some corporate archeology to explore and educate yourself about your company's structure and history. By learning about the various factions of your company, identifying your own personal goals, and becoming clear about what you want for an outcome, you can devise a plan that will increase your visibility within your company and increases your chances for advancement.

Learn about your company. Ask questions and find reading material that explains its history and corporate philosophy. Study its mission statement and learn what that mission means in relation to your own particular job function. By exploring and studying this vital information, you will begin to understand the reasons why your company is structured as it is, and see where you fit into that puzzle.

There is a treasure-trove of historic information about the individuals who founded your company. Take the time to learn their names and stories. Here is the story of Raymond Albert Kroc. You say you don't know Raymond Albert Kroc? Read on.

The popular hamburger chain McDonald's was started by Raymond Albert Kroc. In 1954, at the age of 52, he invested his entire life savings to become the exclusive distributor of a milkshake machine called the Multimixer that could make five shakes at once.

Ray received an order for eight of his Multimixers from two brothers who owned a popular restaurant called McDonald's in Southern California. Ray wanted to meet his new customers, Dick and Mac McDonald, who had a need to make 40 milk shakes at once, so he headed west. When he arrived in San Bernardino, California, he saw that the McDonald brothers were easily serving many people at once and realized that if they opened multiple restaurants like the one they had, he could sell eight more of his Multimixers to each one of them. Ray asked them about that prospect, and Dick McDonald responded, "Who could we get to open them for us?" Ray responded, "Well, what about me?"

Ray opened his first McDonald's in Des Plaines, Illinois, a year later in 1955, and today the Golden Arches are among the most recognized trademarks in the world.

Here are some suggestions for creating your game plan. Use each step as a rung on your corporate ladder and you'll find your way to the top.

- As you begin your detective work to unearth information about your company's past and current position in the marketplace, study its organizational chart to learn about its various divisions and departments. Keep a file and add articles and press releases on these divisions and departments for reference. Ask questions and build your own database regarding your company and its interests and activities.
- After you have explored the history and skeletal structure of your company, begin to put names to those in various leadership positions on the organizational chart. Learn

about those leaders and discover what function they serve within the company. Try to put faces to the names of those in senior management positions so when you meet them, you will recognize them and be able to call them by name. Web sites, annual reports, and corporate press releases often show pictures of senior-level managers.

- After you've determined the names of the individuals in the various positions in your company's key leadership roles, begin creating a dossier on them. Become aware of their management styles and how their personalities interact with those around them. Listen carefully and note their strengths and hot buttons. Learn about their personal and professional histories, and if possible, know their philosophies and goals in relation to the company.

- Study or create your own job description with the help of your manager or supervisor. As you see what's expected of you, you can satisfy those requirements and even excel at them. If you don't know what your superiors expect of you, you risk falling short of the mark.

- Build relationships with those around you and always deliver your best work. Learn when it's best for you to shine, give others credit, step in and help, or leave people alone to succeed or fail without your fingerprints on their work.

- After you've studied the profiles of the leaders in your company, choose one of them to become your mentor. Ask this individual to have lunch or meet you after work for coffee (once a year, a quarter, or month) to answer questions and give you guidance on your professional goals. It's your responsibility to pay for the lunch or coffee and always remember to thank your mentor for his or her time.

- Last, but certainly not least, determine where you want to go in your company and find out what you need to do or learn to get there. Knowing your internal career path is vital in helping you get where you want to go, and it's information that's imperative to your success. You won't know those answers until you have accomplished the thorough investigative process described above.

Your Strategy for Success

ISSUE

You've decided to outline a plan to advance within your company. What are a few of the things you can do to begin your plan?

SOLUTION

➤ Borrow information from your human resources department to learn about your company's founders and early history.

➤ Study the organizational chart and put names to faces of the leaders within your company.

➤ Learn about the people in leadership positions in your company.

➤ Make the decision to work toward a specific job within a specific amount of time. For example, vice president in charge of sales for the western region within three years.

➤ In order to reach that goal, create a game plan of corporate visibility and choose a mentor within the company to guide you along the way.

➤ Study the description of the specific job you've chosen and begin to take any necessary educational classes that will help prepare you for it.

Using Your Soft Skills to Raise Your Personal Profile

As you begin your networking strategies within your company, you'll need to create a personal visibility campaign to show how truly diplomatic and indispensable you are to your management. Learn to put the spotlight on yourself by using your soft skills while remaining humble in your efforts, and you'll rise high in the ranks of your organization.

> "So let us begin the work we were hired to do and leave this a better place than we found it."
>
> —PRESIDENT GEORGE W. BUSH, SPOKEN DURING THE ADDRESS TO HIS NEWLY SWORN-IN WHITE HOUSE STAFF, JANUARY 22, 2001

Breast-beating and lauding your efforts through bragging or obvious self-promotion will make you seem like an opportunist who is not a team player and an overly ambitious oaf who is only out for yourself.

✔ Checklist: Your Personal Visibility Campaign

❑ *Deliver your work on time or early.* Leadership is based on the discipline of being a self-starter and working at a pace that creates timely results.

> "A problem well stated is a problem half solved."
> —CHARLES F. KETTERING, INVENTOR AND SCIENTIST, 1876–1958

❑ *Never reveal a confidence.* High levels of professionalism involve dealing with sensitive information. If you are not capable of holding private information, you will not be trusted to perform meaningful jobs for your company.

❑ *When you meet the various leaders in your company,* greet them by introducing yourself (refer to Chapters 1, 2, 3, and 4) and saying that you're pleased to meet them.

❑ *Never make promises you can't keep.* Don't overpromise or underdeliver. Only tell people what is possible. It is better to underpromise and overdeliver.

❑ *Stay focused.* If you allow yourself to take personal calls, read personal e-mails, or chat incessantly with those in your office or industry, you are depriving yourself of the gift of focus. The more focused you become, the more work you produce and the more you will be valued by your management.

❑ *Give credit to others.* Work is a collaborative effort. When you receive information from people who have helped you do your job, thank them. After you have done your work, make sure you give credit to those who made it possible. Thank people often and let them know you appreciate them and their work.

❑ *Stay organized.* If your desk, office, and computer are littered with files and information, but you can't immediately find that information, then you are wasting your and your company's time. Create a system that offers instant access to information. Your desk and office are a reflection of what's going on in your mind and personal life.

❑ *Create trust among your associates.* Treating them with utmost respect and dignity shows your ability for diplomacy. Even if associates don't do their job to your satisfaction, don't berate them; help them if you can. If they are incapable of doing their job, speak to your manager privately and ask for advice on dealing with these associates.

❑ *Do exemplary work.* Go that extra mile and strive to constantly improve by asking for feedback, thoughts, and opinions from your manager and associates. It's easy to get into a rut and lower the standard of your own work by not asking if there are areas where you might improve.

❑ When you're working in a team to complete a project, you must be willing to:
- Communicate because team work is always a collaborative process that requires diplomacy;
- Depend on your team members and allow them to depend on you to achieve your objectives;
- Stay focused (like a laser beam) on your team and individual results;
- Allow yourself to disagree but prove your reasons rather than relying on gut hunches;
- Quickly overcome any conflicts that arise;
- Remain flexible and yet continually reassess your objectives;
- Practice active listening skills;
- Provide your teammates with support and give credit where it is due;
- Assign and deliver tasks until you complete your project;

- Celebrate the completion of small tasks along the way and reward yourself and your team for your benchmarks of progress.

❑ *Never complain.* A person with a positive attitude rises in leadership. If you're tempted to complain about anything (including the traffic or weather) stop yourself and find something positive to say. People avoid others who complain. No one likes to hear your negative comments. A professional is pleasant and positive at all times.

❑ *Be well groomed.* This may seem obvious, but grooming and hygiene are important to your professional success. Dress well. Keep your fingernails clean. Comb your hair and check yourself in the mirror at least once during the day to see if you need any quick repairs. Keep a toothbrush in your desk to use if you have garlic or spinach at lunch. Polish your shoes. Keep your eyeglasses clean. If necessary, use dandruff shampoo.

❑ *Be aware of your own annoying habits.* Most habits are unconscious, and you may not even know you have them.

- Avoid interrupting people when they're speaking to you.
- Don't bring in daily sagas about your personal life. Avoid updating your co-workers about disagreements with your spouse/partner/children/parents or your health problems or financial woes.
- Focus on others in conversations and avoid talking about yourself too much.
- Keep your hands to yourself. Don't touch people unnecessarily in the workplace.
- Don't talk too loudly. Keep your voice low so work can occur around you.
- Avoid the use of sarcasm—that only pushes people away.
- Avoid overusing humor. Not everything is a joke. Like sarcasm, overuse of humor pushes people away.
- Monitor your moods and park Mr. or Ms. Grumpy at the door.
- Chew and pop your gum when you're at home, not work.

- Please, be aware of your body odor. Bathe daily.
- Keep your desk area or office organized and avoid leaving piles and stacks of paperwork and files in view. It makes you appear disorganized and incompetent.
- Avoid the use of heavy colognes or aftershave.
- Don't curse at work. It shows you have a limited range of vocabulary and emotions. In other words, cursing makes you look like an angry adolescent who's in a huff and having a tantrum.

The 3 Cs heard in the rooms of 12-Step Program Al-Anon[1]
You didn't Cause it.
You can't Control it
You can't Cure it.

- Don't offer personal advice to anyone unless it is asked for. It may come as a surprise, but nobody likes to hear unsolicited advice. This is a bad habit.
- Deliver work that is above average. Strive for excellence.
- Don't lie.
- Be on time or ten minutes early. Yes, it can be done.

To learn what habits are annoying to others, ask for feedback. Is this easy? No, but you must know the answers to advance in your company.

---

[1]Al-Anon provides hope and help for family and friends of alcoholics. For a list of meetings in your area call your local chapter of Alcoholics Anonymous, or visit www.al-anon-alateen.org.

Raising Your Profile

ISSUE

The president of your company approaches you and says, "You've done an excellent job on the reports I've been seeing from your department." What do you say in response to thank and offer credit to your associates?

SOLUTION

You reply, "Thank you. It was a collaborative effort on the part of many people in my department, including Betty Billon, Louise Letty, and Steve Stewart."

ISSUE

If you want to create a positive profile within your company, what can you do?

SOLUTION

Be a person capable of collaborative teamwork and deliver quality work on time. Avoid complaining, and when you speak, choose positive and encouraging comments in all areas.

Your Personal Publicity Campaign

> "Fame is the perfume of heroic deeds."
>
> —SOCRATES, 469–399 B.C.

A campaign for highlighting your diplomacy skills and humanity takes time and effort but can offer great rewards. Perhaps you think your job doesn't provide the opportunity to catch the eye of senior managers in your company. However, it is possible to draw attention to yourself by stepping outside your job function and participating in company-sponsored projects.

- Volunteer for the charity your company supports. Some companies offer employees a few hours of paid time off each month for volunteer work in certain predetermined nonprofit areas. Ask your human resources manager if such an opportunity exists and if so, volunteer.

- Write an article for your department outlining the steps and time line for a project in progress. If your department doesn't currently have a monthly or quarterly newsletter, ask your manager if you can create and circulate one to highlight projects and people.
- Find out if your company offers employee activities such as summer picnics; a baseball, tennis, or bowling team; holiday outreach and holiday parties; or community development programs. If so, ask how you can volunteer to work on a committee that organizes these activities, then participate and enjoy yourself.
- Many companies donate time, money, or employee resources to special needs in the city where they are located. A company may sponsor a sporting event, a local sports marathon to support disease or disaster relief, or the building of homes for Habitat for Humanity. Find out if your company has these volunteer opportunities and if so, sign up. If such a program doesn't currently exist, find out how to start one.
- You might also create visibility for yourself by volunteering to teach a particular expertise you have to others.

CASE STUDY 12

Highlighting Your Diplomacy Skills and Humanity

ISSUE

You want to create visibility that reveals your level of humanity in your workplace? What do you do?

SOLUTION

Your company is sponsoring a community-based project at a local charity. You send an e-mail to the person organizing the event and volunteer to participate next Saturday afternoon.

Perhaps you can lead a class in how to play chess, build a Web site, make jewelry, grow herbs, or tap dance.

||||||||||||||||||||||||||||||||||

CHAPTER SUMMARY

★ Create a game plan for your ultimate goals.

★ Use your soft skills to raise your personal profile.

★ Organize a personal visibility campaign to highlight your skills, diplomacy, and humanity.

Office Protocol During Delicate Situations

> "Life can only be understood back-wards; but it must be lived forwards."
>
> —Søren Kierkegaard, Danish philosopher and religious writer, 1813–1855

I N THESE CHANGING TIMES, THERE ARE unspoken rules of diplomacy for sensi-tive and delicate circumstances in the workplace. This chapter explores many of those hard-to-handle situations that are difficult to talk about.

Cubicle Behavior

Whether your office is a square cubicle on the floor of a large insurance company or it's along mahogany row next to ten partners in your accounting firm, sometimes you just can't get far enough away from people's irritating habits and behaviors. What can you do if you're trying to concentrate and all you hear is the person at the next desk on their speaker phone, popping chewing gum, cracking their knuckles, and slurping coffee? If you're like most people, you'll say nothing until one day, when your nerves are raw, you explode with something mean and nasty that you later regret. Instead of waiting for your steam to build, say something now and do it with kindness. The person with the irritating habit may not even know they're bothering you. In the meantime, you can try to lead by your good example. Cubicle habits that create good will include the following.

- Avoid using computer sounds for your keystroke functions, for example, a sound that announces the arrival of e-mail.
- Don't use your speaker phone when people put you on hold and there's music playing.
- Please, clip your fingernails at home, not work.
- Don't argue with your spouse where others can hear you.
- Go to the washroom to blow your nose or cough deeply.
- Take any personal conversation that lasts more than three or four minutes from your cubicle to a conference room.
- Clean your cubicle after eating at your desk to avoid attracting bugs.
- Wear a headset if you listen to the radio.
- Avoid cursing or spreading gossip.
- Don't lie for any reason. Your associates will not respect you when they hear you lying. Don't do it.

✔ Checklist: Dealing with Irritating Behaviors

- ❑ Look for ways to deal with the annoyance before you speak to the person.
- ❑ When you do speak to the offender, make sure no one can hear your conversation.
- ❑ Try speaking to the person in a conspiratorial tone (almost a whisper) as if to infer, "This is personal and important."
- ❑ Practice what you'll say before you speak. Then say something like "Marty, I know you like to listen to the news headlines

online, but did you know I can hear it when I'm on the phone with clients?"

Constructive Cubicle Advice

ISSUE

The person in the cubicle next to you has a bad habit of conversing over the speaker phone throughout the day. This is very noisy and distracting when you're working at your desk since you can hear both sides of the conversations. What do you do?

SOLUTION

Go to your neighbor in the cubicle and kindly say that you can hear entire conversations and would appreciate it if he or she would wear a headset and speak more quietly. Chances are your neighbor will apologize and agree to comply with your requests.

What About *Your* Habits?

To learn whether or not you have irritating office behaviors, ask the people around you to tell you. You may be surprised to hear you have your own cadre of habits such as bad breath, noisy jewelry, complaining, messy reports, or strong perfume or after-shave. Be prepared to listen to your associates without becoming defensive. Try to take their comments seriously and not hold a grudge against them for telling you the truth.

Dealing with Sarcastic People

Sarcasm is a ploy to keep people way. According to *Webster's Revised Unabridged Dictionary*, the word *sarcasm* comes from the Greek word meaning to tear flesh like gods, to bite the lips in rage, to speak bitterly, a cutting jest. Sadly, sarcasm runs rampant

> "Sarcasm is the language of the devil, for which reason I have long since as good as renounced it."
>
> —THOMAS CARLYLE, HISTORIAN AND HUMORIST, 1795–1881

throughout our modern culture and is a poor substitute for humor. There are some people who try to make a punch line out of every interaction you have with them. Everything's a joke, and they'll make you the target of that joke whenever possible. Try to speak to sarcastic people in a serious tone about a sensitive subject, and they usually tear it to bits with sharp comments they think are funny.

There are two good ways to deal with sarcastic people. First, ignore their sarcasm and don't rise to the bait. After all, they use sarcasm to avoid intimacy and keep people away. If you get caught in the net with sarcastic people, do your best to give them what they want, which is to be left alone.

Second, once a person crosses the line and becomes abusive with their sarcasm, be calm, look at the person directly and say, "I don't appreciate your sarcasm, and I would like it if you would not be sarcastic when you're speaking to me." After your comment, walk away.

CASE STUDY 14

Dealing with Sarcastic People

ISSUE

You have an office associate who constantly makes fun of all those on the company baseball team. Your league has a last-place ranking, and you're sensitive about it. What do you do?

SOLUTION

When this associate comes by your office and makes a sarcastic remark about the game the previous evening, try saying, "We played our best. I resent your sarcasm, and I would appreciate it if you would avoid using it when you're speaking to me." You get up and walk out of your office and leave the person standing there alone.

Death of a Co-Worker—Funeral Etiquette

The expected or unexpected death of an associate requires a gesture of respect to the family from those in your office. It is always appropriate to send condolences. Expressions of sympathy help you and the family's loved ones process the grief that arises during this time.

> "I feel we are all islands—in a common sea."
>
> —ANNE MORROW LINDBERGH, PILOT AND AUTHOR, 1906–2001

All religions and cultures have their own acceptable funeral rituals based on the faith of the deceased. If you do not know how to honor the loss of a business associate, contact the funeral home, the deceased's house of worship, or a family member to learn about the best ways to show your respects. For example, it is common to offer the family of a deceased Buddhist gifts and vegetarian food instead of flowers.

✔ Checklist: Acknowledging the Death of a Co-Worker

❑ Most obituaries in local newspapers will tell you whether there will be services open to those who would like to pay respects to the family of the deceased or private ones for family only.

❑ The obituary may also give instructions to people who want to express their sympathy. For example, the announcement may say "The family asks that instead of sending a gift of flowers, donations be made to [a charity, church, medical research group]," or "Flowers may be sent to the Elm Street Funeral Home," or "Flowers may be sent to the Peace Way Cemetery."

❑ You may send sympathy cards to the family of the deceased but choose simple, nonreligious ones unless you're sure of the family's faith. Many people at your office may sign the card.

❑ In case you hear about the death of your associate at the office, ask the person giving you the information what is known about the funeral services. If the person doesn't know anything, help make the arrangements for someone in your office to call the family on behalf of the deceased's co-workers. This person should tell the family member she or he is calling to inquire about funeral arrangements and should express sympathy to the person who answers the phone.

❑ Be sensitive to the family members of your associate when you attend the funeral. Family members at funerals are often so preoccupied with their thoughts about their loss that they can't hear the words you say to them. It helps for you to express simple yet emotional condolences, such as "I will miss her," or "John was my friend," or "My sympathy."

❑ Do not be afraid to mention the deceased employee's name at work. Everyone grieves in their own way and communication lessens the sadness. However, if your own grief persists, seek professional help.

CASE STUDY 15

Expressing Sympathy and Support

ISSUE

Your boss has invited you into her office to tell you that one of your office associates was killed in a car accident on his way to work that morning. What is the protocol for expressing sympathy to the family?

SOLUTION

You know from what the deceased associate's family member told your boss that funeral services will be held on Friday at 10:00 A.M. at the Main Street Funeral Home. You were very close to the deceased and so make arrangements to attend the services. Your company sends a floral arrangement to the funeral home. Everyone in your immediate office signs a sympathy card to send to the deceased's wife and children.

Personal Phone Calls

Most employers accept the fact that their employees may place or receive one or maybe two calls a day of a personal nature; however, three or more calls during a business day are considered unacceptable.

Here are some suggestions for dealing with personal calls during work hours.

> "Everyone thinks of changing the world, but no one thinks of changing himself."
> —LEO TOLSTOY, RUSSIAN AUTHOR, 1828–1910

- Carry a beeper with you so your family and friends can leave you a voice-mail message on it. They can also punch in their number in case of an emergency. When you return their calls, use a pay or personal cell phone.
- Try to have your own cell phone. You can collect messages and return calls during breaks. Avoid constant use of your cell phone during business hours. You're there to focus on your company's business not your personal life.
- If you do make or receive calls on your phone at your desk, be quick and get back to work as soon as possible.

CASE STUDY 16

Managing Personal Phone Calls

ISSUE

You have a small child who is at day care but is often sick. How can your child's day-care worker contact you when necessary?

SOLUTION

Wear a beeper.

Yawning

Yawning is contagious. Doing it in someone's face shows your lack of consideration for other people. If someone walks into your office and yawns widely, chances are, you'll yawn right back. According to scientists, yawning is a human behavior related to boredom or sleepiness; it is possible to stifle a yawn. Perhaps you're yawning at this very instant just after reading about it.

The following are suggestions for dealing with your own yawning.

- If you're sitting at your desk where people can see you and you find yourself tempted to yawn, take a break, a walk, and a few deep breaths.
- Take a trip down the hall to the privacy of the washroom instead of yawning in front of your associates.
- Cover your mouth and practice stifling your yawn.

CASE STUDY 17

If You Get Caught Yawning

ISSUE

You're bored. The report you're working on requires tedious and monotonous number-crunching. You're just about to stretch, open your mouth, and yawn when your boss walks in your office. What do you do?

SOLUTION

Stifle your yawn by breathing through your nose with your mouth closed. Stand up quickly to show respect and try to wake yourself up a bit.

Bluntness

"To say nothing, especially when speaking, is half the art of diplomacy."

—WILL DURANT, AUTHOR AND HISTORIAN, 1885–1981

While some top executives may get away with being blunt and to the point in their business dealings and are even applauded for their effective management style, mere mortals who try the same behavior are usually labeled as rude. Being blunt and unemotional when delivering pertinent information is the least effective communication style you can use. Bluntness is perceived by people as a condescending attitude that is tinged with a lack of caring; it triggers intimidation or a defensive stance from the listener.

✔ Checklist: Avoiding Bluntness

❑ Practice active-listening skills by acknowledging, repeating, validating, and reflecting the speaker's comments (see Chapter 5).

❑ To be an effective communicator, you must demonstrate a high level of compatibility with people. Your communication suffers when your bluntness causes a serious break in the dialogue.

❑ Practice using visual and descriptive words. Relax. Ask questions and listen to the answer.

❑ Use open body language (open arms, smiles, uncrossed arms and legs).

❑ Ask for feedback from your listener.

❑ Offer encouraging comments and offer sincere compliments instead of dumping information or giving directions (or orders) to your listener.

CASE STUDY 18

Communication vs. Bluntness

ISSUE

Your client has invited you to his office to discuss a recurring problem he's having with your company, and he is very angry with you. You are tempted to tell the client the problem wouldn't recur if his company provided you with the proper documents. How would you handle it?

SOLUTION

You listen to your client, tell him you understand, and ask questions to clarify the problem. You might even compliment him by saying kind things about his

---

CASE STUDY 18, CONTINUED

company and products. After developing a decent level of communication, you begin telling him about the need for proper documentation to assure the problem doesn't occur again. Your client hears you and understands his company's role in the process. You are successful in your communication without resorting to bluntness.

‖‖‖‖‖‖‖‖‖‖‖‖‖‖‖‖‖‖‖‖‖‖‖

CHAPTER SUMMARY

★ When faced with the death of a co-worker, or an associate's family member, determine the way(s) you and your office should show your respects by calling the funeral home, the house of worship, or the family.

★ Don't simmer about an irritating behavior exhibited by someone in your office; tell them about it and ask for their cooperation to minimize it.

★ Make as few calls from your desk phone as possible. If you need to make or receive more than two personal calls per day, wear a beeper or use a pay or personal cell phone.

★ Stifle your yawns.

★ To avoid bluntness, practice active-listening skills and make efforts to appear friendly.

Business Meetings

ONCE YOU CAN LEAD A SUCCESSFUL business meeting, you're on your way to being promoted into a leadership position in your company. By successfully leading a meeting, you reveal a variety of aspects about your basic character. Regardless of your academic accomplishments or your job-related skill level, meetings show your ability to deal with people by using your soft skills. The combination of your job skills and effective relationship skills gives you a decided advantage for recognition within your company. After all, business meetings are arenas where people relate to one another with civility and respect for the direct purpose of accomplishing a particular agenda.

If you develop a reputation for being a dull, antagonistic, untrustworthy, or uninformed leader, your meetings will be attended reluctantly and sporadically. Anyone who uses those same negative characteristics as a meeting attendee won't be invited back. Whether you're attending a business meeting or leading one, you need to understand what's expected of you.

Meetings are to be taken seriously. They are carefully designed to create a highly focused atmosphere that is conducive for conducting business. However, there is an obvious paradox at play here: In this highly focused and serious atmosphere, you are expected to use your soft skills to participate. No wonder few people enjoy business meetings and complain they are too frequent, long, boring, and accomplish little. Without knowing the best strategy for participating in or leading a meeting, it can be easy to believe you should dumb down and park your brains at the door in order to appear savvy. Actually, the opposite is true. The mere fact that a leader invites you to attend a meeting indicates she or he believe you have a valuable contribution to make. Your role as an attendee is to use your diplomacy, finesse, and civility to make that contribution.

Your personal meeting manners are contingent on various factors ranging from the industry, size of the company, geographic location, and even the personalities of the management. What might be considered appropriate behavior in a small advertising agency in Venice, California, is very different from what is expected within a large bank in downtown Boston, Massachusetts. *Normal* is determined by your company's corporate culture.

Meeting Leader Techniques

Leading a successful meeting is a formula that can be duplicated. Here are the five components vital for creating a successful meeting.

1. Create the agenda.
2. Determine exactly what you want for an outcome in the meeting.
3. Don't harp on the problem you're trying to solve; instead, always focus on solutions.
4. Identify and assign necessary tasks to those in the meeting.
5. Accomplish the agenda.

> "Leadership is the art of getting someone else to do something you want done because he wants to do it."
>
> —Dwight D. Eisenhower, 34th President of the United States, 1890–1969

Ten Techniques for Leading a Successful Business Meeting

1. Provide advance notice of the meeting to your attendees. Everybody's busy, and since meetings take time and energy during a normal business day, advance notice is vital to assure a good attendance. Small, informal, inner-office meetings require less notice, but your associates will still appreciate knowing about them ahead of time so they can arrange their schedules. A one-week notice is a thoughtful consideration for people from other departments who are invited to a meeting. Give people coming from out of town two weeks notice so they can make travel plans.

2. Immediately after your meeting, jot down brief notes about what transpired. You might leave out important details by waiting to do this later. Send your manager or superior a brief e-mail covering the major points you covered in your meeting. Your manager may also direct you to send the meeting notes to all those attendees or those unable to attend.

3. Soft drinks, coffee, and snacks are great enticements to lure people to your meetings. It's common today to see announcements or agendas saying, "Refreshments will be served 15 minutes before the meeting." This gives your attendees a chance to arrive early and get a snack before the meeting starts.

4. It is your role to introduce any new guest to the group. You may simply give their name to a large group (10 or 15 people). However, if the guest is a client, board member, or senior executive, try to tell them the name and title of each person in the room.

5. People who already know one another don't need name tags. However, it's courteous for everyone to wear name tags when there's a guest present. Remember, the majority of people are visual communicators, and seeing a name in print helps them memorize it.

6. Try to use words while facilitating the meeting that indicate unity and show positive enthusiasm. Examples are we, us, can, you, will, yes, success, the next step is, please, thank you. Avoid using negative or condescending words such as no, won't, dumb, can't, wrong, stupid, don't, never, shouldn't, and impossible.

7. The best time of day to hold a meeting is 10:00 A.M. This midmorning time allows attendees to stop by their office, have a cup of coffee, and check their phone and e-mail messages first. The least favorable times are Monday morning before 8:30 A.M. and Friday afternoon after 4:30 P.M. It is also unwise to plan a meeting involving a major decision that cannot be made in a brief time too close to lunch when people are hungry and perhaps irritable because their blood sugar is low.

8. Allow a quick break in any meeting that lasts more than 70 minutes to give attendees time to take care of biological needs, check phone or e-mail messages, and return calls, get more coffee, or socialize. Be considerate of the fact that business is still going on despite the importance of your meeting, and people need time to stay plugged into their routines and responsibilities.

9. Leave a few minutes for people to interact during your meeting. Be careful, though, not to lose control and let too much table talk eat up the time you need to complete your agenda.

10. Reassure your attendees at least once during your meeting that you will do your best to end the meeting on time. This subtle reminder is one way to stay in control of your agenda.

Scenario Setup: Leading a Successful Meeting

The following scenario setup shows you how to organize, lead, and execute a departmental meeting with 20 of your peer associates; Ms. Baxter, your immediate manager will also attend. This meeting was called to discuss the four changes in the Jones account.

> "A speech has two parts. You must state your case, and you must prove it."
>
> —ARISTOTLE, *RHETORIC*, GREEK PHILOSOPHER, 384–322 B.C.

➤ Five days before the meeting, you create your agenda and e-mail a copy to those 20 people you've invited to attend.

➤ Two days before the meeting, you send an e-mail reminder to the 20 people to confirm the meeting time and location. You also reconfirm the meeting room, arrange for coffee to be brought, and print extra copies of the agenda.

➤ It's now the day of your meeting, and you stand near the doorway with a confident smile and greet your guests by saying, "Hello. Thanks for coming." You also shake hands with a few people you haven't seen lately. You have extra copies of the agenda near the front of the table for anyone who didn't bring theirs. You invite your attendees to sit wherever they want, except in one predesignated chair on the far side of the room that is saved for your manager, Ms. Baxter. All the department's associates know each other, so no one is wearing a name tag.

➤ When Ms. Baxter arrives, you invite her to sit in the chair you have saved for her to your right at the top edge of the table. Any person who sits to your right (whether you're seated or standing) is always considered a guest of honor at a business meeting or dining table. If there is more than one important person in the room, you may invite them to sit next to or across from each other. The exception is when these important people do not like each other; then you do not want to place them facing each other. Instead, seat them side by side and put a person between them so they don't have to look at or speak to one another directly throughout the meeting.

➤ Wait for three minutes after your designated time to begin the meeting. This allows your guests time to arrive, take their seats, chat, get coffee, and also accommodates various watch settings.

➤ You now stand before the seated group and introduce yourself. You greet your guests and give the purpose/reason for your meeting and a comment about the agenda.

➤ After you begin your meeting, two latecomers enter quietly into the room. You do not stop your meeting to greet them or repeat what's already been covered.

➤ You then tell your attendees what outcome you want from your meeting. For example, "We're going to identify the four changes that affect the Jones account."

➤ Now is also the time to invite your attendees to follow a few basic meeting rules. Make the rules broad and generic and announce them in a friendly tone that will ensure people's cooperation. You might say, "I would also like to ask your cooperation, please. Turn off your cell phones and beepers. There's coffee in the back; please help yourself but do so quietly to avoid disrupting the meeting. We've got a lot to cover in an hour. Thanks."

➤ In case your audience seems uncomfortable, ask what's going on. The room may be too hot, or people may be having a problem hearing you. It's up to you as a leader to make your audience comfortable.

➤ You have the four changes for the Jones account on a flip chart or in a PowerPoint presentation that you carefully prepared before the meeting. Each one of the four changes appears in a different color and on a separate page. Try not to spend more than five minutes on each slide or visual graph since most people have short attention spans and will become impatient and want to move on.

➤ When people start complaining about the problems with the Jones account, you put your open hand up with the palm facing out. This is a universal, nonverbal signal indicating **STOP**. Then you say, "We're not here to complain. We're here to find solutions. Now, who has a solution?"

➤ Toward the end of your meeting, you repeat in a few short sentences what you have said regarding the four changes in the Jones account.

➤ You also take the time to identify and assign tasks and ask for volunteers. For example, someone needs to take the Jones' accountant to lunch to explain the changes, and someone needs to lead the next meeting in two weeks.

➤ You summarize what's transpired by quickly highlighting the changes on the Jones account.

➤ The last ten minutes of your meeting are for questions and answers. One attendee's question takes too long to address and risks running your meeting past the scheduled time; you agree to meet privately with the individual.

➤ You repeat each person's question back to them so they know you heard it correctly. Then you answer in a way that is brief and affirmative. When you don't know the answer to a question, you tell the person you'll get back to him or her once you find it out.

➤ At the end of your meeting, you thank the people who have accepted tasks, offer your final comments, and thank everybody for attending.

➤ Once the meeting ends and you've said goodbye to everyone, you put the room back in its original order, return to your office, and prepare a quick report while your mind is fresh about what occurred in the meeting. Bullet the notes to yourself and send a brief report via e-mail to Ms. Baxter. You also ask Ms. Baxter if she'd like you to e-mail a report to the meeting participants or those who were unable to attend.

The Code of a Good Meeting Leader

A good leader meets the following criteria:

- Allows many people to share and discourages any one person from dominating the meeting.
- Takes charge of the room and assumes the leadership role to create and control the agenda.
- Creates order so that when people speak, the entire group hears them.
- Stays on the track of the agenda and doesn't allow too much small talk at the table.
- Reaches a formal consensus on the meeting's agenda.
- Doesn't allow too many interruptions to short circuit the momentum and progress of agenda.
- Creates a tight agenda that stays on track and runs on time by discouraging people from going off on unrelated topics.
- Is after the truth that impacts the issues on the agenda and doesn't allow it to get buried or ignored by participants who are too intimidated or shy to tell the truth.
- Makes sure attendees leave the meeting with specific directions and know exactly what they need to do.
- Coordinates the attendees' efforts to create results.
- Respects the time of those attending and doesn't pull them away from their desks too often or long.
- Allows enough breaks during the meeting.
- Makes sure the meeting was valuable and creates results.
- Doesn't plan a meeting too close to lunch when every-body's hungry.

✔ Checklist: When You're Attending a Meeting

❑ Greet the meeting leader (handshake optional) when you enter.

❑ If you're a junior officer in the company, don't assume you can sit anywhere. Wait until others have taken their seats or ask the leader where you should sit.

❑ Avoid talking to attendees about subjects not related to the topic of the meeting.

❑ Don't whisper or criticize during the meeting. No complaining is appropriate. You're there to create solutions.

❑ Always put your briefcase on the floor and not on the table.

❑ Be concise and participate with informed and helpful contributions but do not ramble.

❑ Stay on track and stick to the subject on the agenda.

❑ Never resort to ranting on any subject. Remain optimistic and realistic.

❑ Be punctual for the start of the meeting and your return after breaks.

> "Brevity is the best recommendation of speech, whether in a senator or an orator."
>
> —CICERO, GREAT ROMAN ORATOR, POLITICIAN, 106–43 B.C.

❑ Keep both feet flat on the floor at all times. Avoid sprawling, yawning, or allowing your eyes to dart around the room.

❑ Keep your cell phone and beeper turned off.

❑ Show your total attention to those speaking by sitting up straight and focusing on them with direct eye contact.

❑ Arrive prepared and follow through with any tasks you agree to do.

❑ Smile. Appear pleasant and engaged, regardless of who's speaking, what the topic is, or how long the meeting goes on.

❑ Do your homework ahead of time and know enough about agenda topics to be able to contribute.

❑ Take notes when appropriate. Ask questions to clarify any points of confusion.

❑ Throw away any trash that accumulates during breaks and at the end.

❑ Thank the leader after the meeting (handshake optional).

CHAPTER SUMMARY

★ Meetings are held to brainstorm, educate, inform, solve problems, comply with procedure, reach a consensus, encourage creativity, and identify and assign tasks.

★ The five basic components of a business meeting are: 1) deciding the purpose and creating an agenda; 2) defining the intended outcome; 3) solving problems without complaining; 4) assigning tasks; 5) completing the agenda.

★ As a meeting facilitator, your job is to define the purpose and reason for the meeting, prepare and accomplish the agenda, choreograph the agenda to produce results, and keep people informed.

Mastering Corporate Politics

"I don't wait for moods. You accomplish nothing if you do that. Your mind must know it has to get down to earth."

—PEARL BUCK, AUTHOR, 1938 NOBEL PRIZE WINNER FOR LITERATURE, 1892–1973

YOU MAY THRIVE IN AREAS THAT REQUIRE political maneuvering or wither like the Wicked Witch of the West when doused by a bucket of water. Office politics can include the good, the bad, and the ugly of anyone's professional life. Just the word *politics* sounds shrouded in dishonesty, mystery, and shady behaviors cloaked in egotism; however, that's an incorrect image. Once you accept the fact that politics exist in the workplace and learn to become politically adroit through relationship management skills, your career track will take you to the top. Knowing when and how to use manners and etiquette skills to become a master diplomat in an ethical way when dealing with politics will enable you to thrive. Learning the rules to the game of *relationship management* is the core of office politics. Once everyone acknowledges that politics are a part of business, your office will become an enjoyable place to work. Turn a blind eye to that fact and avoid managing office relationships to your advantage, and you'll lose. It's that simple; it's your choice.

Ten Steps for Winning at Office Politics

1. Never Let Your Enemies Know Who They Are

Once again, you are confronted with your willingness to act in a way that demonstrates your adaptability to remain professional and respectful to all people despite the circumstances. Stand close to your enemies, and your presence will be welcomed in all circles. Learn to control your emotions and never harbor or show ill will toward anyone, and you will gain the respect of your associates. Observe the captains of industry today, and you will see that many of them may dislike people within their company or industry but have learned to keep their personal opinions to themselves and surround themselves with people they trust implicitly to accomplish their personal goals and the goals of their companies. The more people who trust you and appreciate your value, the quicker you will rise in the ranks.

CASE STUDY 19

Showing Honor

ISSUE

Your boss, J.L. Smith, and other senior executives are standing in the middle of a room. You dislike J.L. Smith and don't agree with his ethics, relationship management skills, or politics. However, he is your boss, and for you to advance in your company, he must trust you and respect your skills. What can you do (not say, but do) to show your deference to him?

SOLUTION

You subtly mirror his gestures, smile, listen to him, and when he speaks, you turn slightly in his direction (see Chapter 2). Please note, this does not mean you say

---

or do anything wildly incongruent with your own belief system. You simply demonstrate signs of respect for your boss and his position through a variety of nonverbal gestures that create visible yet subtle signs of rapport with him. Remember, your political success is determined by your ability to exhibit high levels of self-awareness and self-control.

2. Discover Who Considers You an Enemy and Build Bridges

You must take risks to succeed in business; occasionally your ideas and your business style will create conflict for you for an hour, a week, or longer. It's important to know if you have any enemies and then organize a calculated campaign to win them over by building bridges in areas where you can find agreement. But first, you must learn the exact reasons your enemies have chosen their adversarial stance against you and address those issues.

Spend face-to-face time with your enemies whenever possible. This adds a touch of humanity that cannot be found by speaking with them on the phone or through e-mail. By sitting down and discussing your commonalties and differing points of view, you may be able to work through the issues that affect your working relationship. Your willingness to mend any damaged connections for the good of your company is another political skill that prepares you for a leadership position.

CASE STUDY 20

Turning Enemies into Allies

ISSUE

You have overheard that Martha Meyers considers you her enemy because of a decision you made on the Newell account. You enter the office dining room and see that Martha Meyer is having lunch with three of her friends. What steps do you take to restore that relationship?

SOLUTION

- As you enter the dining room, you walk directly to Martha Meyers's table, greet her, and tell her what a great job she has done on the Newell account. You also ask her if you might schedule some time with her to get her advice on dealing with the account. She agrees to a meeting later in the week.

- When you speak to her the next day to arrange a convenient time for your meeting, tell her she has much to teach you and you appreciate her willingness to take the time to walk you through what she knows about the account.

- When you have your meeting, take the opportunity to find common ground and agreement on a variety of subjects before you approach the Newell account.

- Once you begin to discuss the account, show her your respect. Martha candidly admits she has been upset with you because you overrode a decision she made. Tell her you'll do what you can to consider her suggestions and reassure her you'll send her updated reports so she will know your progress.

- Ask Martha if you may drop by her office the following week for ten minutes to show her your progress and see if you're implementing her suggestions to her satisfaction. As a result of your diplomacy, Martha is pleased, and you turn an enemy into an ally since now she has a stake in your success.

3. Know Who Your Allies Are and Show Them Respect

Make a list of individuals in your company or industry who are important to you. This list will shift over time, but for now, include people you consider politically important to you and your career. This means those with the power to promote or teach you something. Acknowledging this list will enable you to begin a positive relationship management campaign with each person.

Be lavish in your praise of your allies, quote things they've said when they're standing next to you (and remember to give them credit), and defer to them because of their position or your genuine feelings of fondness or respect for them. Ask for time with them regularly and make sure you find ways to stay on their radar screen. Go that extra mile and do favors for them, show an honest interest in them as people, offer to assist their efforts, and show enthusiasm for your alliance.

CASE STUDY 21

Showing Respect

ISSUE

Stoney Stoltz is standing with ten other young executives in your company, and you have come to meet him. You have heard that he is the most powerful man in your company and that he enjoys spending time with young executives to groom them for future leadership positions. What steps do you take to create a relationship campaign with Stoney?

SOLUTION

- Smiling, you approach him, wait your turn, introduce yourself, and join in the group conversation. After 30 minutes, you ask Stoney if he might grant you a half-hour appointment in the near future to answer some important questions you have about the company. He agrees and immediately sets up a time with you. You are grateful and thank him and let him know how much you respect him.

- The day before your meeting, you call his administrative assistant or send an e-mail to confirm the appointment. You arrive at the meeting with him with prepared questions and write down his answers in front of him. You ask if he will agree to meet you again in six months (or a year). He agrees.

- When you get back to your office, you send him a quick thank-you note via e-mail or traditional mail. A handwritten note on nice stationery or a card is much warmer and shows more consideration than e-mail.
- You do your homework and find out that Stoney's birthday is in two months. One week before that date, you mail him a birthday card. On the card, you mention the good advice he gave you and the outcome of that advice.
- Three months later, you see an article related to your conversation in a magazine or online and mail or e-mail it to him.

These small personal gestures are called *pings* and are your relationship-building tools for quickly creating a positive history with Stoney that will deepen your rapport with him. When you see him next time, he will mention your gestures of kindness and will have a commonality for discussion since you've quickly created a history for your new relationship.

4. Never Tell Lies

Telling the total truth and being a person of your word is an admirable goal worth striving toward. Wouldn't business (and life) be easier if you could say "Yes," when you mean yes and "No," when you mean no?

Business doesn't always operate through total and complete disclosure. There are many times when you will (and should) not fully answer all the questions people ask you. Understand that honesty becomes habitual and is a trait worth developing, but you don't need to tell everything you know at all times. To do your job effectively and avoid lying, it may be best to be vague and ambiguous at times with your comments. For example, if you are asked, "Are you on board with us?" and you have serious reservations about your total commitment, respond by saying, "I understand what you're trying to accomplish and your need to have everyone on board; I'll do my best to be supportive." If you are unwilling to make a commitment when someone specifically requests it, you have several options for what to say.

- "I understand what you're talking about, and I'd like to know if you have considered these consequences?"
- "I hear what you're saying. Who else has fully committed to this?"
- "I see the problem you have. Did you see the Laker's game last night?" (Yes, it's a blatant example of avoidance, but it shows you how the deed is done.)

Beginning each sentence with "I understand," "I hear," or "I see" makes the person think you're agreeing with them when you are not. You simply acknowledge that you were listening and heard what they said. This technique for avoiding the need to tell lies or commit to something you're not willing to do is called *agree and redirect*. By definition, you are finding something you can agree to (even if it's only stating that you heard what the person said) and then redirecting the conversation and attention by changing the subject. Agree and redirect protects you from giving false information and puts you in control of the person and conversation. This technique has its place in business but should be used sparingly and diplomatically, or you will be accused of being a slippery character who avoids giving direct answers.

CASE STUDY 22

Agree and Redirect

ISSUE

Nine of the associates in your department are gathered in a tight circle in the center of the room when you enter. You know the department is being down-sized and four of your associates in this group will be laid off. They don't know which ones will be leaving, but you do. What do you do with such information?

SOLUTION

As you approach the group, one of your associates says to you, "Do you know who's being laid off?" And you say, "The timing couldn't be worse for this lay-off. It's a good thing the job market is good right now."

5. Learn to Listen and Avoid Talking about Yourself

Knowledge is power. It is best to keep your private life very private. Having a few friends at the office is a desirable goal, but not everyone will turn out to be your best friend. When most (though not all) people are speaking to you at work, they only want to talk. Sadly, many people ask questions but only want brief answers from you so they can talk. People without balance in their personal lives often use the workplace as the outlet for discussing their problems, and they can be tiring to be around. If you must speak about your private life at the office, be generic and avoid details that provide too much information.

People who give you too much personal information during work hours and continually bring in their dirty laundry about fights they've had with their spouse, their drug use, a rumored extramarital affair, their depression, their divorce, or their serious financial problems, will eventually impact your productivity and faith in their ability to do their job. You have one choice and one choice only with these energy-draining vampires. You must say to them, "I realize you're dealing with some difficult issues, but you may need to get professional help. I don't have time to listen." While this comment may sound harsh, it's your only choice so that your productivity and effectiveness will not suffer and impact your company's success. In case you feel you can really help this individual, do so after work.

Note that relationship management and political skills also include sincere demonstrations of deep compassion and gestures of celebration for others. Tragedies and great events do occur in people's lives; when they do, reach out and offer your support; just do your best to keep your job responsibilities in the forefront.

Your private life from 5:00 P.M. to 8:00 A.M. (or whenever your off hours are) is your time to develop balance and prepare yourself to be more productive in your job. Your off hours are your time to enjoy your family and friendships, rest, educate yourself, worship, volunteer, shop, enjoy hobbies and interests, exercise, and take care of your home and health.

CASE STUDY 23

Remain a Private Professional

ISSUE

Your associates are drinking champagne at an office party. Their conversation turns to the topic of bad habits they have when they're at home. The discussion becomes too personal and revealing; now you know who's staying up all night surfing for a new job on the Internet and who's addicted to video porn. When you're asked about your bad habits, what do you say?

SOLUTION

You give a minor transgression that keeps you in the loop of the conversation without denigrating yourself or offering too much information. You tell about a bad habit that doesn't reflect on your character such as, "I occasionally leave my receipts at the ATM machine." Keep your sharing generic and unmemorable unless it supports your reputation. It is far better to be thought of as dull than to tell people about any flaw or weakness that might diminish your good character.

6. Reveal Only the Cards You're Meant to Reveal

The higher you advance on your company's corporate ladder, the more access you'll have to privileged information. You may use that information wisely or to practice covert and deceptive political office games for gain. Top-secret information is a privilege awarded by your company, and it is your job to use that information to empower those around you and build relationships. You should also share the information with those who need it. Using secrets to play people against one another and experience the underbelly of power will inevitably backfire on you.

Reveal only the cards you were meant to reveal. It is your duty to keep private any confidential information that will harm anyone or do damage to your company. When someone wants information you don't believe they should have, say, "I know you'll understand, but this is not public information. If you are directed to share private information, tell them, "I am entrusting you with this private information for your purposes. It is not public and may not to be told to others."

CASE STUDY 24

Hold Confidences

ISSUE

You know that your company management is talking about merging with another company and that many jobs will be lost in the process. You want to tell your administrative assistant that your and her job are not secure, and management has given you permission to share this confidential information. How do you handle this?

SOLUTION

You say to her, "I want you to know that I believe you are a good administrative assistant and you have highly marketable skills. I am going to give you highly classified information: Our company is merging with another, and we may or may not have our jobs in 90 days. This is private information for you only. Management knows I am telling you this, and I am asking you to keep it confidential while the leadership of the company makes their plans to publicize it to all employees."

---

7. Act Decisively Once the Final Decision Has Been Made

Making decisions is generally a collaborative process that reaches a climactic moment and is then followed by a specific set of actions. When it's your turn to act, do so bravely and without complaint or fanfare.

- Create documents that are clear and directive and support your decision to act.
- Memorize the key points in your directive to act. Repeat these key points often to those who need to be reminded.

- Before acting on the decision, take the time to brief your allies to gain their support.
- Prepare your enemies with timely information so they will not be alarmed.
- Encourage questions within all ranks to diminish dissension, rumors, gossip, or complaining.

CASE STUDY 25

Act Decisively

ISSUE

Senior management has given you the responsibility of delivering the unpleasant news that there will be no year-end bonuses to those in your department. You realize that sharing this news will put you in an unfavorable position. How do you handle this?

SOLUTION

You do not procrastinate but move quickly and professionally to deliver the information.

- First, you call a meeting of those who report to you and give them all a one-page report outlining the issues you've been asked to cover.
- You explain the unpleasant news, make sure everyone understands each facet of the issue, and invite questions regarding any lingering points people may have.
- Once you are satisfied people understand the issues, you ask them to prepare a modified version of your one-page report to pass along to the associates in their departments.

---

8. Keep Your Company's Best Interests in the Forefront at all Times

Your personal contribution to your company is vital to its success. Although the employee manual may not have noted *loyalty* as a characteristic in your job description, your employer assumes you want your company to succeed and prosper. In order for that to occur, you are called upon to remain positive about your company's prospects and make verbal and written comments that demonstrate your loyalty and dedication. If you are in conflict with the business's ethics or products, then clearly, you are working for the wrong company and should find a job that is a more suitable match for your skills and talents.

CASE STUDY 26

Remaining Loyal to Your Company

ISSUE

An associate calls you and says, "Hi. I just found out our manager's going to be out of the office all day Tuesday. Let's take a four-hour lunch and tell everybody we're making sales calls." How do you respond?

SOLUTION

You say, "I can't. I'm working on an important report that's due on Wednesday." You don't give a moral lecture but simply let the associate know the company and its business are important to you.

---

9. Know Your Company's History and Philosophy

Innovative individuals started most companies by identifying a need in a marketplace and then manufacturing and delivering a product or service to satisfy that need. But there is always more to the story. Often, the personality and culture of a company's origins remain in place to this day and are reflected in its philosophy.

When a company employs you, take the time to know the story of its early roots, its founders, and the joys and struggles of its early associates. By educating yourself in this way, you are deepening your commitment to your company's efforts.

Knowing Your Company's History

ISSUE

During a low time in the economy, the office morale is low. You want to do your part to brighten your associates' attitudes. What do you do?

SOLUTION

You conduct research and learn about the individuals who founded your company. You tell your associates about the personal sacrifices and courage they exhibited when they founded the company 20 years ago and point out the wisdom of their perseverance. The associates will feel a renewed sense of pride and loyalty for their job and company.

10. Offer Encouragement and Help to Those Who May Need It

Use your skills, talents, and contacts to offer help to others freely without any attachment to the outcome. Remember that relationship management and political diplomacy are based on creating strong alliances. You were hired for your specific set of skills and should use them to help others through rough spots when necessary. These same people will no doubt help you when you need their skills. True relationship management expertise in the workplace is knowing when and how to offer your help and support.

Offering Encouragement

ISSUE

An associate tells you with dismay that he doesn't have time to oversee the next departmental meeting. What do you do?

CASE STUDY 28, CONTINUED

SOLUTION

Offer to lead the meeting for your associate by saying, "I'll be glad to lead the meeting for you."

||||||||||||||||||||||||||||||||||

CHAPTER SUMMARY

★ Never let your enemies know who they are.

★ Discover who considers you an enemy and build bridges.

★ Know who your allies are and show them respect.

★ Never tell lies.

★ Learn to listen and learn to avoid talking about yourself.

★ Reveal only the cards you're meant to reveal.

★ Act decisively once the final decision has been made.

★ Keep your company's best interests in the forefront at all times.

★ Know your company's history and philosophy.

★ Offer encouragement and help to those people who need it.

Diplomacy and Personal Accountability

A FFICIONADOS OF CORPORATE-SPEAK CAN be overheard talking about consumer loyalty because they know the value of retaining their customer base. Research shows that it costs businesses five times as much to find a new customer than to keep a satisfied one.

Upon closer examination, human decency and high levels of respect are codes of compulsory business conduct that help encourage customer loyalty and satisfaction. By learning a few skills related to diplomacy and personal accountability, you can create goodwill with everyone, everywhere you go.

> "I think a compliment ought to always precede a complaint, where one is possible, because it softens resentment and ensures for the complaint a courteous and gentle reception."
> —MARK TWAIN, AMERICAN WRITER, 1835–1910

Delivering Compliments

> "When envoys are sent with compliments in their mouths, it is a sign that the enemy wishes for a truce."
>
> —SUN TZU, CHINESE MILITARY STRATEGIST, 430–400 B.C.

Delivering sincere compliments is your opportunity to practice an enjoyable and productive facet of business. As you move up in your career, you'll have many opportunities to use flattery as part of your professional rapport-building toolkit. However, you must know when and how to use these tools, or you'll be perceived as a lightweight charmer who prattles on and on for attention and personal gain.

No two people require the same quality or degree of praise for their efforts. Some people need infrequent and private praise, while others need regular doses and enjoy receiving it in front of other people. There's nothing wrong with these "unlicked cubs" that regular flattery won't cure unless they require inordinate amounts of reassurance or praise; then it's not your responsibility to accommodate their needs unless you enjoy doing so. Which one of your clients or office associates (there are always a few) needs extra attention? Having this knowledge will help advance your career.

How and When to Give Praise

The golden lesson for getting people to do what you want them to is to reward the *behavior you wish to encourage.* This also applies to your Labrador retriever at home. Praise someone (or some pet) when they do something that pleases you, and they will (unconsciously) strive to continue to do it. Your bonus comes when they strive to improve in other areas in an attempt to please you again and continue receiving your praise.

The more you praise others at the appropriate time and in the way they like, the more they will *want* to please you.

In a business world that encourages political correctness in the workplace, complimenting your associate's, client's, or superior's personal appearance is unwise. You may, however, compliment job performance by saying, "You did an excellent job creating the graphics for the report," or attitude by saying, "I appreciate your patience."

Tell people *exactly* what area you're complimenting. Instead of saying, "Good job," find something particular such as, "I really liked the references you provided to back up your assertions."

Be timely with praise. Giving it prematurely or waiting too long diminishes its effectiveness.

Offering praise via e-mail is common, but it packs more punch when delivered in person. E-mail is meant for transmitting nonemotional information only. You'll learn about e-mail etiquette in Chapter 16.

Receiving Compliments

People who consistently receive compliments are those who contribute to their company, department, and community. They are generous with their time and talent, and people thank them often.

> "A person places themselves on a level with the ones they praise."
>
> —GOETHE, GERMAN POET AND AUTHOR, 1749–1832

Generally, people who receive compliments are also those who give compliments to others. These people receive and accept compliments graciously instead of dismissing the praise offered by the giver. This makes the giver more likely to offer praise again since a sense of satisfaction is received for the complimentary efforts.

Two Behaviors that Kill Compliments

People who are ungracious to the person giving them a compliment won't receive another one. For example, someone says, "Thanks for getting the report to me on time," and the other person replies, "It could have been better. I just threw it together." The person who delivered the compliment will feel embarrassed, as if their opinion had no value.

The other extreme is when the person receiving the compliment is overly prideful; this diminishes the value of the compliment. Say someone offers a compliment by saying, "Thanks for getting the report to me on time," and the other person replies, "Getting it to you on time nearly killed me. I worked on it until midnight for a week." This type of comment makes the giver want to take back the compliment. An ideal response would be "You're welcome."

Behaviors that Encourage Compliments

When someone offers you a compliment, let the giver know you appreciate it. Simply saying "Thank you," is always appropriate, especially when you make eye contact with the giver as you say it.

When you are given a compliment, deliver a kind or flattering comment back to let the giver know how much the appreciation matters by saying something like "Thanks, Sue. Coming from you, that compliment really means a lot to me," or "Thank you for taking your valuable time to tell me that," or "Thanks. It pleases me to know that it meets your high standards."

CASE STUDY 29

Giving and Receiving Compliments

ISSUE

A customer thanks you for finding a lost invoice by saying, "Thanks. If you hadn't found this lost invoice, my account would have been past due in three days." How do you respond?

SOLUTION

You say, "You're welcome. We really appreciate having your company as a client of ours."

ISSUE

An associate helped you prepare a report for your manager, and you want to thank the person. What do you say?

SOLUTION

"I just heard from my superior. The report you helped me with was a hit. That section on shipping data was the clincher with those graphs and charts you prepared. You really did a great job. Thanks."

CASE STUDY 29, CONTINUED

ISSUE

Your boss gives you a compliment that makes you very happy. He says, "You are amazing. You really saved the day for me. I took your report into the meeting and after all the arguing stopped, I gave them a copy of your report, and they had to concede my point. Thanks." What do you say in response?

SOLUTION

You stand and smile and you say, "Thank you. The fact that you took the time to tell me this in person means a lot."

How to Handle Criticism

Constructive criticism is an oxymoron. How can you be expected to accept criticism as helpful and constructive? Whether it comes from your boss or a client, there is a distinct difference between criticism and good critique. Criticism is directed at you as a person and openly charges you with flaws in your level of intelligence, judgment, and character. Critique is a review of your performance or behavior that is intended to offer you support and helpful feedback and assist you in your job.

> "Criticism is an indirect form of self-boasting."
> —Dr. Emmet Fox, writer and speaker, 1886–1951

Listen carefully to a client's criticism and respond calmly without emotion to the complaint. If this does not seem possible, ask your superior to step in and help the client.

Listen carefully to a client's criticism and respond calmly without emotion to the complaint. If this does not seem possible, ask your superior to step in and help the client.

Criticism from an Office Associate

Criticism from an associate is uncalled for in any work environment, and it can leave you feeling demoralized and alienated. Everyone (from those in the mail room to the top floor of management) is vulnerable to some form of criticism in working life, and it always stings. If you're lucky, you'll have a manager, supervisor, and work associates who critique your work in a way that offers constructive feedback and doesn't affect your self-confidence or impair your future working relationship with them.

Few people receive loud and caustic criticism well. Such persistent criticism can lead to feelings of abuse, anger, fear, and disgrace. All people work best when there is a base level of respect and mutual trust among their associates; breaking that level of trust degrades the person being criticized and harms their future work and working relationships.

✔ Checklist: Dealing with Inner-Office Criticism

You may not like the following suggestions for dealing with criticism, but they are appropriate and diplomatic responses in line with the highest benchmark of professional conduct.

❑ Listen to what your criticizer has to say. Allow the person to speak uninterrupted unless he or she begins to rant or use vulgarity or insults. In cases where criticism develops into verbal abuse, you have every right to say to your abuser, "We'll discuss this further when you can speak to me like a professional," and then walk away.

❑ Even though you may feel a person's criticism of you or your work is unmerited, she or he is still entitled to express it *if* it is within the range of professional comments.

❑ Most people are ill-equipped to deliver criticism and make it a mutually beneficial conversation, so when you're the one being criticized, it's your role to be the more skillful individual in the interaction. The best way to diffuse criticism is to practice active-listening skills. State that you hear and understand your criticizer and tell them you'll do your best to make changes.

❑ If you receive consistent verbal criticisms from the same individual over a period of weeks or months, you may be dealing with a person incapable of applying professional behavior with you. In this case, you should address the harm this person is doing to your self-esteem and may even consider changing jobs if you are unwilling to allow such constant criticism.

❑ Keep an official journal to record these criticisms. Include dates and specific examples. Such a paper trail may prompt an investigation and mediation or some other option to stop the criticism. Keep the comments in your journal unemotional and don't mention the personality traits of the person who is criticizing you. In other words, don't say anything that could be considered name-calling or caustic such as "He's such a jerk" or "She's a dork." Record only the facts of the incident. In case this situation escalates to a legal issue, your journal and all your e-mails could be subpoenaed as evidence in a court of law.

CASE STUDY 30

Dealing with Abusive Criticism

ISSUE

Your immediate supervisor begins screaming and throwing insults and criticisms at you in front of other people about a report you turned in two weeks ago. He is out of control, and you actually feel afraid for your personal safety. What do you do?

SOLUTION

You listen and then say, "I understand you're unhappy with the report I submitted to you two weeks ago. When you're not upset, I'd like to find out exactly what

CASE STUDY 30, CONTINUED

needs to be changed and I'll make the corrections to the best of my abilities. I would appreciate it if you would not scream at me in this way." Your supervisor continues with the verbal abuse, and you say, "I would like to discuss this report at a time when you're capable of speaking to me with professionalism." When you get back to your office, make a note in your journal that clinically and factually (without emotion) describes the specific elements of the incident and date it.

Humor and Joke Telling

"The tragedy of life is not that we die, but is what dies inside a man while he lives."

—ALBERT SCHWEITZER, MEDICAL MISSIONARY AND PHILOSOPHER, 1875–1965

A good sense of humor is a highly esteemed and admirable trait that demonstrates much about your personality. A good laugh helps you relieve stress and gives you energy. Humor also brings people together during the workday and creates camaraderie that helps to break workplace tension. Top management is wise when they instill some humor into their corporate culture and allow a degree of levity to be included in their meetings and public image. Do your part to be pleasant. Everyone enjoys being around those who are capable of an occasional smile now and then.

Jokes are a public X-ray of your true character. Listen carefully, and people will tell you everything about their character through their jokes. All you have to do is tell a single joke that picks on any particular group of people, and you will quickly define yourself as prejudiced, narrow-minded, and racially, sexually, or ethnically biased. Much of today's humor is mean spirited and takes jabs at religious denominations, gender, sexual orientations, or nationality stereotypes.

Learn to tell at least three good jokes. Choose them wisely and practice timing and delivery with your family and friends before using them in public. Learn to tell your jokes with flair and end them properly with a well-rehearsed punch line. In case you're not a joke teller or the jokes you enjoy are not appropriate for the workplace, memorize a few humorous quotations to insert into conversations to illustrate your sense of humor. There are many within this book and quote books in libraries and bookstores.

CASE STUDY 31

Using Quotations for Levity in the Workplace

ISSUE

Your associates are commiserating about a client's indecision, and you want to bring a bright comment into the conversation. How do you bring a quote into the conversation to add levity?

SOLUTION

You might say, "Maybe we've given our client too many options. To quote Albert Einstein, 'A man with one watch knows what time it is. A man with two watches is never sure.'"

ISSUE

Your associates are complaining about the difficulty of an upcoming task. What do you do to encourage them by using a quote?

SOLUTION

You could say, "We can do this. As Walt Disney once said, 'It's kind of fun to do the impossible.'"

ISSUE

Your company lost a major account to a competitor, and your associates are upset. How do you use a quote to cheer them up?

SOLUTION

You could say, "Well, it's true. We did lose that account. But we learned a lot and we'll make up the loss on the next one. As the great general George Patton once said to his troops, 'Success is how high you bounce when you hit bottom.'"

Dealing with Frustration or Anger

"You will not be punished for your anger, you will be punished by your anger."

—BUDDHA, FOUNDER OF BUDDHISM, 568–488 B.C.

In the past, business climates often tolerated displays of anger and even hostility in the workplace; employees followed wrathful leaders out of fear, not respect. Today, public or private displays of anger from the senior management level are no longer accepted and will (without exception) damage an executive's career. Great leaders have found personal ways to control themselves and deal with their frustration and anger. Executives must have high levels of self-control in order to be leaders, and for this reason, the business community recognizes them as extraordinary people and lavishes them with demonstrations of respect (and often big salaries). These leaders may experience high levels of frustration and anger but have learned how to deal with these intense emotions without allowing them to interfere with their relationships, productivity, or health.

Dealing with your own extreme emotions of frustration and anger can be exhausting, especially if you're doing your best to keep a lid on them and control yourself at work. By shutting yourself off from your true emotions, you risk low levels of concentration, poor work performance, and possibly impaired health. You must find a way to raise your tolerance level for frustration and anger or you will risk suffering from physical ailments such as ulcers, high blood pressure, heart problems, and depression. Even though you may think you're masking your emotions, your clients and associates can sense your anger just below the surface and intuitively know that you're a walking kettle ready to boil over at any moment.

✔ Checklist: Managing Your Frustration and Anger

❑ Accept the fact that your work can often be frustrating and cause you to feel angry. Admit that you occasionally feel these intense emotions. Denying them could cause your anger to come out sideways through sarcasm, snide comments, cursing, belittlement of others, and regular rants on a variety of unrelated topics. Accepting you have frustration and anger is the first step in learning to control them.

❑ Get physical exercise: go to the gym, walk around the block after lunch, or participate in a sport. Do anything that releases stress from your body and mind. Or go to the other extreme and join a yoga class, turn off the television and radio and practice meditation, or sit in silence and practice your own form of prayer.

❑ Your parents were right when they taught you, "Count to ten before you react." When you feel tempted to deny your emotions or act out your frustration or anger, stop, acknowledge that you feel angry, and count to ten. Reevaluate what you want for an outcome before you express your anger and count to ten again. Do your best to appear to turn into an ice statue until you can to react in a professional way.

❑ Keep a private journal at home as a purgative tool. Pour out your frustration and anger onto the page and then, at the end of your ranting and raving, give yourself some advice or a pep talk about the situation. Keeping a journal gives you a safe place to blow off steam without endangering your career or hurting yourself or those around you. Allow your journal to be as raw, emotive, and explosive as you'd like. You may even tear out the pages and destroy them after you've written them, but allow yourself the freedom of exploding on paper. The more you journal, the more you will learn to detach from your internal turmoil. *The New Diary: How to Use a Journal for Self-Guidance and Expanded Creativity* by Tristine Rainer is an excellent book that teaches journaling (see reading list at the end of the book).

❑ Never lash out at anyone. No circumstance warrants the loss of your self-control. Ever.

❑ If you are frustrated and angry beyond the point of reason, you may need professional help to guide you to the answers that will help you diminish and resolve your problems.

Without such help, you risk damaging your professional career, intimate relationships, and health. You deserve to feel emotional freedom, and remember, no one likes to be around a hothead.

CASE STUDY 32

Keeping Your Cool

ISSUE

You've been invited to join a meeting with the president of your company. There are also six senior-ranking officers in attendance. This meeting has been called to discuss whether or not to close your division, and you could lose your job. How do you handle yourself in the meeting?

SOLUTION

Although you are frustrated, angry, and on the verge of exploding, you sit through a three-hour meeting on the subject of closing your division. You sit quietly, count to ten, acknowledge to yourself that you know you're angry and frustrated, reexamine what you want to occur in the meeting and your desired outcome, and then make a conscious decision to be calm and in control of your emotions. You count to ten again. You slowly take out a pad and quietly make a few notes that you will elaborate on in your journal after the meeting. When you are asked questions, you answer them to the best of your ability without showing your superiors your anger and frustration. After the meeting, if your feelings of anger and frustration are still at a peak point that may lead to explosive behavior, you seek professional help from a top business coach (Colle Davis at www.mycoach.com) or a counselor.

Office Gossip

Gossip damages the reputation of the person being gossiped about and, to a lesser degree, damages the reputation of the person who spreads it. Gossip can be entertaining when it passes along positive and interesting information, but it is dangerous when it demeans or endangers another person's character. Once you develop a reputation as a gossip within your company, those in positions of leadership will avoid giving you sensitive, confidential, and timely information, and you will be shunned by those in circles of power and influence. Gossip takes away from the business at hand and steals time and productivity from your company as surely as stealing money from the office's petty cash drawer.

Gossiping becomes a habit like any other daily behavior. While the image of people enjoying congenial chats around the water cooler may conjure up pictures of laughter and harmony among your associates, it's not always that way. As soon as people in your group begin maliciously gossiping about others in your office, they take the chance of damaging their career as well as the career of the person being gossiped about; that is when gossip becomes an unacceptable professional behavior.

> "Great minds discuss ideas. Average minds discuss events. Small minds discuss people."
>
> —Navy Admiral Hyman G. Rickover, 1900–1986

There are times when passing along some salacious tidbit about someone seems too tempting to keep to yourself, so you whisper it with a conspiratorial admonition, "Don't tell anyone, but . . ." After three or four people have shared the same information, the original story gets diluted by half truths and exaggerations and invariably, someone gets hurt.

People gossip about others because they think that having information and passing along a hot scoop gives them some kind of power only known to insiders. Gossiping about others also keeps an individual from looking at themselves and their own life. Those who gossip may be bored, petty, immature, or just nasty people who enjoy passing along information about other people's weaknesses, foibles, and idiosyncrasies. They need an audience to satisfy their desire to draw attention to themselves as they trash others. Listening and providing such people with an audience makes you guilty of having the same weak character they have.

What to Do with Office Gossip

ISSUE

You're standing near the water cooler, surrounded by a dozen of your office associates, and someone says to you, "Did you hear about Tillman in accounting? He's getting demoted because he's got a drinking problem." What do you say in response?

SOLUTION

You finish drinking your water, do not acknowledge that you even heard the comment, say nothing, and leave the group without comment.

|||||||||||||||||||||||||||||||||||

CHAPTER SUMMARY

★ To stop receiving compliments, be ungracious to the giver.

★ To elicit compliments, say thanks and return them.

★ Praise others often and tell them why.

★ Learn to critique and not criticize people's work.

★ Joke telling is a public X-ray of your true character. Reveal the best of yourself.

★ Accept that you feel anger and frustration and control these emotions.

★ Gossip can hurt. Don't do it.

SECTION III

CLIENT SERVICES

Networking

> "Fools look to tomorrow. Wise men use tonight."
>
> —Scottish Proverb

THERE IS A DIFFERENCE BETWEEN NET-working and selling. Networking is your plan for meeting people and developing business and social contacts. Selling is the act of offering a fee-based product or service to a person or a company. Those in networking circles know the difference between networking and selling, and it's important that you learn it, too, if you want to be accepted into networking circles.

Whether you're self-employed or representing a product or service for your company, effective networking is mandatory in America's competitive business climate. There are new rules for the 21st-century model of networking; the old one of *suit up and show up* seems naive compared with today's sophisticated one of spreadsheet relationship management.

Everybody's doing it. At least, successful people are doing it. Those who are in sales, management, and leadership positions have identified the networking niches that work for them and committed to maintaining and nurturing their contacts over a long period of time. However, because people enjoy routine and going to the same events to see friends, it's easy to fall into a rut and become comfortable with your networking group instead of expanding your horizons beyond the people you already know. Such a rut does not defeat the purpose of networking, but it does limit your possibilities.

Eight Good Reasons to Network

1. Create and maintain business contacts.
2. Make friends and have fun.
3. Learn about other people's lives, interests, and businesses.
4. Generate visibility for yourself and your company.
5. Educate people about your product or service.
6. Meet your competition.
7. Find opportunities to serve on a committee and become a part of a group.
8. Help people make connections with contacts you have made.

"Whatever you do, do it with all your might. Work at it, early and late, in season and out of season, not leaving a stone unturned, and never deferring for a single hour that which can be done just as well as now."
—P.T. Barnum, creator of "The Greatest Show on Earth, ®" 1810–1891

As you glance over the "Eight Good Reasons to Network," you'll see that each one requires the use of your soft skills to develop and maintain. Please consider implementing a 90-day networking campaign in your life to meet new people at events, on the phone, and by e-mail. At the end of 90 days, you will have built a new and exciting database of contacts, friends, ideas, and projects, and your life will be forever changed since you'll see the world differently once you've begun this adventure. First, however, you may need to change some current habits since many networking events take place in the evenings. Though you'll be sacrificing many of your evening hours for 90 days, the rewards are far greater than any inconvenience you experience.

Attend a networking event with the idea that you're there on a relationship crusade to get to know people and let them get to know you, and you'll be more relaxed and have more success and fun. Try not to go with a *hungry* look in your eyes since people will sense your desperation and go out of their way to avoid you. Once people sense you're there only to collect as many business cards as possible or to try to sell them something, they won't trust you or introduce you to people in the group. Professionals know the new rules for successful networking, and it's best you learn those rules or you'll strike out the first time you get up to bat.

Find a Room to Work

It takes a certain level of humility to network. After all, you must continually put yourself *out there* in new situations with many people you don't know and who don't know you. To avoid burnout or disappointment, choose your networking meetings carefully. Find a group that matches your criteria. As you begin your search, ask yourself, "Why am I going there?"

> "The person who goes farthest is generally the one who is willing to do and dare. The sure-thing boat never gets far from shore."
>
> —Dale Carnegie, author of *How to Win Friends and Influence People*, 1888–1955

If You Can Answer YES to Any or All of These Questions, Then GO

Are you going there to:

- Meet decision-makers who might *eventually* buy your product or service?
- Meet people who might *introduce* you to decision-makers who may eventually buy your product or service?
- *Learn* about a facet of your industry from successful people who are at the forefront?
- *Teach* other people about a facet of your industry and create visibility as an expert in your field?

- Have fun and meet interesting people?
- Serve the group and become part of its organization?

Once you decide to embark on a 90-day networking campaign, attend a minimum of two events each week to get your feet wet and begin to develop your contacts and relationship management campaigns. You can go at your own pace, of course, but keep in mind you're only searching for a few groups that fit your criteria for networking.

Even seasoned networking professionals are only looking for highly-qualified candidates that fit their profile for developing a management relationship campaign. An ambitious yet reasonable goal would be to meet and cultivate 50 qualified candidates in one year. That number will vacillate when some candidates become dormant or unresponsive due to their schedules or else become your clients. Try to add four or five individuals per month to your roster and work on a relationship management campaign with each one of them.

Many professional people in large and small cities across America choose networking as a lifestyle. Each week, they attend as many as 10 to 15 events, such as business meals (breakfast, lunch, and dinner) lectures; fundraisers; association, board, chamber of commerce, and planning meetings; panel discussions; business or country club social events; and business-related sporting activities such as golf or ball-games.

> "Circumstances!?! I make circumstances."
> —Napoleon Bonaparte, emperor of France, 1808–1873

The Four Secret Keys for Attending Networking Group Meetings

1. You're not at a networking event to sell an individual anything. You can do that later. You're there to meet people and develop relationships with them.

2. Go to events your potential clients are attending. If you're a widget salesperson, and you want to meet people to buy your widgets, join a group or association where there are

people who can make decisions about buying widgets or know others who can. Don't attend too many widget gatherings of other widget salespeople. They don't need your widgets; they have their own.

3. After you have identified a networking group or association and attended a few of their meetings, find out who belongs and who attends. Groups often have members who attend only occasionally but are important people to know. Target a few individuals as beneficial candidates for you to pursue and begin a long relationship-development campaign with them.

4. Attend networking meetings to give back, not just take from, the group. Once you identify a group to attend regularly, ask the leaders how you can serve. Is there a committee opening? Is there some task you can perform to add to the success of the group?

✔ Checklist: Creating Your Successful Networking Plan

❑ Study your industry. Interview your family, friends, and clients and create a list of ten people you'd like to meet. Make another "wish list" of ten more people you believe would be ideal candidates for your product or service.

❑ Choose 24 (or more) networking opportunities to attend in 90 days in a variety of arenas and vary their scope. You might choose association meetings, industry meetings or conferences in your area, panel discussions or lectures in a related field, social and charitable groups, and lunches that a friend or associate has arranged. Or mix it up and create your own menu of activities.

❑ Make these meetings a priority in your life by making reservations and noting the date, time, address, and directions in your calendar or personal data organizer.

❑ After attending a few meetings, target one or two individuals you'd like to get to know and research them and their

> "Make voyages!
> Attempt them . . .
> there's nothing else."
> —Tᴇɴɴᴇꜱꜱᴇᴇ Wɪʟʟɪᴀᴍꜱ,
> Aᴍᴇʀɪᴄᴀɴ ᴘʟᴀʏᴡʀɪɢʜᴛ,
> 1911–1983

companies so when you meet them, you can speak intelligently.

✔ Checklist: Working the Room

❏ Wear your name tag on your right shoulder. This makes it easy for people to read as they reach across your torso toward your right shoulder to shake your hand.

❏ Prepare and memorize a ten-second elevator pitch to use with people during the event to introduce yourself, your company, and product or service. For example, "I'm Aaron Stein. I'm an urban interior designer with Grahame and Grahame in Houston. We specialize in remodeling and designing office space."

❏ Prepare and memorize a 20-second elevator pitch to use to tell people your name, your company name, who you work with, what you do for your clients or customers, and how you do it. Create this 20-second pitch in small sound bites that people can hear and remember. Be sure to include the following:

- Your *name.* "I'm Aaron Stein . . ."
- Your *company* name. ". . . and I'm with Grahame and Grahame in Houston."
- A *description* of your perfect client. "Our clients are generally companies in major urban business centers . . ."
- What you *do* for them. ". . . and we create customized interior office spaces . . ."
- *How* you do it, ". . . by designing a space that matches the company's image and the function it serves in the marketplace."

❏ Prepare and memorize a 30-second elevator pitch to use when someone is seriously interested in your product or service. You may never use it, but by preparing it and committing it to memory, you can always use bits and pieces of it as necessary. You can say a *lot* about yourself in 30 seconds;

speaking quickly, you can say 100 words. Even speaking slowly you can say 85 words. Take time to write and practice your pitch.

❑ When someone asks you the popular question, "What do you do?" answer in as few words as possible by addressing the specific niche you and your company serve in the marketplace. Aaron Stein would say, "I design office spaces for urban companies." Your answer should describe the function you perform for an ideal potential customer to every person you meet, and this enhances the value of your networking experience.

❑ Go prepared with three areas of small talk by using the 30-Day Rule.

❑ Don't talk to anyone for more than ten minutes; eight to ten minutes is ideal. You're there to *work the room* not *play*, and if you talk only to people you know or to someone who takes you hostage in the corner, you've defeated your purpose. To end a conversation, simply say, "It was a pleasure meeting you," and depart. If they will not let you go, excuse yourself to the washroom or another destination.

❑ Never linger longer than 15 minutes even when you meet someone you're very interested in talking with. Remember, you're there to network and not monopolize your time or theirs. End your conversation with, "It was a pleasure to meet you. Perhaps we could speak on the phone, have coffee, or get together for lunch in the near future."

❑ Practice the 80/20 Rule. Listen 80 percent of the time and talk 20 percent of the time, and when you do talk, do it pleasantly and speak clearly. Don't ever let a disparaging word cross your lips by complaining about anything (including traffic or weather). No one wants to listen to drivel.

❑ Take plenty of business cards with you and one 3-by-5-inch card to make notes to yourself.

❑ Carry as little as possible to shake hands and demonstrate open body language gestures. Leave your briefcase at the office or in the car. Ladies, carry a small shoulder-strap bag with only your essentials in it to allow you to keep both hands free for gesturing. This is a sign of confidence and dominance, and women can easily use it to make a powerful first impression. You have only a few minutes to make a positive first impression, and it takes 20 positive subsequent impressions to correct a bad first one.

❏ Find out who's organizing the networking event. Call that person, introduce yourself, and ask if they (or someone else) can introduce you to some people attending the event.

❏ Try to find out who will be attending the cocktail party or networking event ahead of time and prepare yourself with information about these people and their companies or interests.

❏ Arrive ten minutes early and study the name tags or badges (if available) on the entry table. If you see the name of someone you'd like to meet, ask greeters at the desk if you may paper-clip your business card to the back of their badge. On the card, write, "I look forward to meeting you tonight."

❏ The people at the desk are a wealth of information. Ask questions about the attendees and ask them to introduce you to someone on the list.

❏ Eat and enjoy a beverage before you attend or early enough in the cocktail party or meeting so you can network the rest of the evening with your hands free to shake hands and gesture. Or you may carry a drink with you in your left hand so when you shake hands with someone, your right hand is not wet and clammy from the sweating glass.

❏ Professional networkers seldom eat or drink past the first 30 minutes of the event; they're too busy *power-schmoozing* and working the room.

❏ Avoid standing near the bar. People may congregate there, but it's not an ideal spot to engage people in conversation. Instead, stand near the food or dessert table where people are lingering and eating. You'll find them more amenable to talking because people like to chat during meals and their blood sugar is higher after they've eaten (this puts them in a good mood).

❑ When food is served at a networking event and attendees are invited to choose where to sit, do not randomly claim any seat at an empty table. Be proactive by waiting until people sit and then picking your table. This way you will make sure you sit next to people you want to meet.

Scenario Setup: Working the Room

➤ You've called ahead and the organizer of the event has agreed to introduce you to a few people. You arrive ten minutes early to meet the organizer.

➤ Imagine you've been told by various people that Pamela Purdue and David Daniels both attend this event regularly. You glance at the front table and see the name tags. You ask the people at the table if you can attach your business card behind their name tags. They invite you to do so. On your business card you write, "Looking forward to meeting you tonight."

➤ After you've looked around the room, you immediately help yourself to a beverage and some food before the other guests arrive.

➤ A stranger approaches you and introduces herself: "Hi. I'm Cindy Parker with The Oakroad Neighborhood Association." You reply, "Hi. I'm Maxine Anderson. I'm with Sold-Sign Real Estate in Lincoln Park." You then turn the focus off yourself and back on Cindy by asking her questions about her job and interests.

➤ You determine after one minute that the communication channel she uses is kinesthetic (See Chapter 6). You say to her, "Cindy, I *feel* so lucky to have met you tonight. Can you find *a quiet moment* to get together to have coffee with me? I *love* driving through the Oakroad area, and you are just the person who can *help me* with some questions I have. May I please have your card?"

➤ You shake hands with Cindy, exchange cards, and give her a sincere good-bye.

➤ As you leave Cindy, you see Pamela Purdue. Pamela is president of the local school district. You approach her and say, "Pamela. It's such a pleasure to meet you. My name is Maxine Anderson. I'm the person who paper-clipped my business card behind your name tag." After a moment, Pamela asks what you do, and you give her a memorized five-second elevator pitch especially tailored for her by saying, "I specialize in helping people with children find homes in good school districts in the area."

➤ After three minutes, you see that many people want to speak to Pamela, so you say, "Pamela, I know you're busy, but may I take you to lunch sometime? I'd like to talk to you more about what your school district offers so I can tell clients about it when they ask me." Pamela agrees and gives you her card. She already has your card.

➤ After you say good-bye to Pamela, you see David Daniels. You approach him and say, "David, it's a pleasure to meet you. My name is Maxine Anderson. I'm a good friend of your brother-in-law, Phil Proctor, and I attached my business card to your name tag." After you have introduced yourself, you ask David questions about himself. Although you are listening carefully to what he's saying, you are also waiting for an opportunity to say that you know his company supports Junior Achievement. David is the president of a national company with local headquarters in the area that hires and transfers people into the home office on a regular basis.

➤ Finally, as the clock ticks toward six minutes, you get your opening and say, "David, I understand your company supports Junior Achievement. May I stop by your office and meet with you sometime? Perhaps there's a way I can help your company's efforts with Junior Achievement." He agrees and gives you his card.

The Networking Thread of Follow-Up

Professional networkers know that the event, meeting, or party they've attended is only the tip of the iceberg. The real work is yet to come.

Relationship management skills are based on long-term efforts. This process is not a one or two swings of the bat approach. Just because you have met these people does not mean they will remember or do business with you. They need to know, trust, and like you, and understand your business style and ethics. The only way to create this relationship is to take a long-range (six months to two years) approach to develop it into a mutually beneficial one.

> "The doer alone learneth."
>
> —Friedrich Nietzsche, German philosopher, 1844–1900

Maxine Anderson, the savvy real-estate lady with Sold-Sign Real Estate, met three people that evening who could give her enough leads to fuel her business. These people are connected and respected in business arenas and at the centers of influence in their community. They are exposed daily to people in transition. The *last* thing Maxine will do is ask them for business before she's sure she has developed an adequate level of rapport and confident they will say "Yes." Please note, every profession and person requires a different level of relationship development to establish rapport for doing business. Be sensitive to this fact and be patient.

✔ Checklist: Following up the Networking Thread

❑ When Maxine got home that night, she sent all three people an e-mail saying, "It was a pleasure meeting you. I'll call you in a few days to set up some time to get together. In the meantime, I'm putting an article in the mail I thought you'd enjoy seeing." Over the next three days Maxine purposely searched on the Internet and through magazines to find information these people might be interested in reading. She sent Cindy an article about neighborhood associations, Pamela one on the rewards and struggles of school superintendents, and David one on the impact his company has had on the local economy. With each article, she attached her business card and a note on her Sold-Sign Real Estate company stationery saying, "Thought you'd enjoy this. I'll call you in a few days to arrange a convenient time to get together. Regards, Maxine Anderson." Then she mailed the letters.

❑ Maxine created a separate file in her system for each of these three people. On the outside of the file she wrote (yes, you can write on the outside of a file) the date and action of each ping she made.

❑ In a week, Maxine sent an e-mail to her list saying she was going to call them tomorrow to schedule a time to get together. She asked if they would take a moment to look at their calendar so they could coordinate a convenient time, and she suggested they let their administrative assistants know of two possible time slots in case they were not available when Maxine called.

❑ The next day, she called and booked three separate appointments.

❑ After she had attended the meetings with each of her contacts, Maxine mailed them handwritten thank-you notes.

❑ Over the next six months, Maxine mailed each of her contacts a newsletter she created on her computer specifically designed with news and business items she thought each of her prospects would enjoy. She also included information about her industry and real-estate business.

❑ She sent the contacts cards for the holidays.

❑ She sent occasional e-mails with pertinent information she thought would interest each person.

❑ Over time, these three people learned to know and trust Maxine as a professional woman and began giving their friends and clients her number to discuss their real-estate needs. In effect, Maxine created three ambassadors to help spread the word of her expertise.

❑ At the end of the year, Maxine had chosen a total of 37 such people for her networking campaign. She spent her most valuable marketing time and efforts choosing and grooming the people on her list.

||||||||||||||||||||||||||||

CHAPTER SUMMARY

★ Networking is not selling. It is meeting people to develop business and social contacts.

★ After you attend networking events, target certain individuals you'd like to develop a relationship with and implement a campaign to that end.

★ If someone asks you, "What do you do?" answer them in fewer than 20 words.

★ When you're speaking to someone at a networking meeting, don't spend more than eight to ten minutes. You're there to work the room and create contacts. You can talk more to them later.

★ Follow up, follow up, and follow up for six months to two years. Don't ask for business until you've developed an adequate level of rapport and feel confident the person will say "Yes."

Techno-Ethics

65 Tips for Etiquette Related to Technology

TECHNOLOGY HAS NOT REPLACED HUMAN interaction in business. Used properly, technology supports good communication as long as those who initiate a message (e-mail, voice mail, fax, cell phone, or beeper) consider that a flesh-and-blood human being is on the other end.

The issues of ethics and etiquette that arise in the area of technology point directly to personal accountability on the part of the person initiating the message. Examples of obvious breaches in ethics are e-mail spam, junk faxes, telemarketing, and junk mail. Recipients of unwanted messages are rising up en masse to demand privacy for themselves in the arena of technology.

On August 8, 2002, the Federal Communications Commission (FCC) issued a fine of approximately $5.4 million to a California company accused of sending junk faxes to companies and individuals who did not request them. The FCC contends the company's faxes are a clear violation of the Telephone Consumer Protection Act that was created to protect people against junk faxes, unwanted telemarketer's calls, and unwanted prerecorded telephone telemarketing calls.

Electronic Mail

There is no such thing as e-mail privacy. If your e-mails can't be read favorably by those on the board of directors of your company, don't send or receive them at your office. Most e-mail systems can be monitored by an administrator who reads all messages that come in and out of your mailbox. Think of your e-mails as public information. And remember that all laws governing defamation, copyright, discrimination, and other forms of written communication also pertain to information in your e-mails.

The effective use of business-related e-mail can be followed by adhering to these guidelines:

1. Be brief. Be polite. Don't talk too much.
2. Don't attempt to deliver emotional or volatile information through e-mail. Since they are not interactive, e-mail messages can hurt feelings, damage reputations, and bruise egos. Don't send e-mails that flame by using language that evokes fear, anger, or other extreme emotions. For example, "You did a lousy job," or "You're in hot water. We'll talk next week."
3. When you've finished composing your e-mail, sum up its contents and place that brief summation in the subject line so recipients can find it again in their inbox or

copy/paste it in another place. For example, "Department Meeting, Friday 10:00 A.M., September 22, Jenkins office."

4. Use single spaces in e-mails but double space between paragraphs.

5. When forwarding messages, use the blind copy (BCC) feature and avoid the copy (CC) feature to keep your recipient's addresses private unless you have a specific reason to share them.

6. Business e-mail addresses should also include your contact phone number, mailing address, and fax. The sig-line is an optional feature within e-mail programs that allows you to create your contact information and include it when you choose. You can also add a link address to a Web site that offers more information.

   More formal e-mails may include both your name and your sig-line. For example:

Thank you very much,

JM Patrick

(followed by a standard sig-line)

OPL Corporation

Executive Vice President of Customer Service

1-555-XXX-XXX

www.wplcorp52.plusone.com

Try to keep your sig-line shorter than four lines. Remember, many people print out their e-mails, and a long sig-line creates the need for more paper, ink, and printing time.

7. Avoid adding a quotation, personal motto, or sentence that sums up your personal message or your corporate mission statement at the end of your sig-line. Many people find extended messages a tedious intrusion of their time to read and print.

8. When you're replying to a particular question or comment in an e-mail, pull out that section by copying and

pasting it between angle brackets (< >). Then respond to the comment on the next line. Many e-mail programs offer a simple feature that allows you to highlight only the text you want to include in your reply; simply highlight and hit reply. For example:

<the Denver conference reservations>

Reservations have been made

<what are the dates?>

The conference is scheduled for October 3, 4, 5.

<when do I get my conference schedule?>

You will receive your conference packet two weeks before the conference.

9. Use the paragraph indent feature in your e-mail program, not the tab key, to make indentations in your messages. E-mail programs vary, and tabs can easily become truncated and leave your margins wildly jagged in transmission. You can check your work by e-mailing a copy to yourself and seeing what it looks like when it arrives.

10. Use attachments only when necessary. Ones that include graphics or require more than about 100 KB (KB means kilobytes and 100 KB is a large file) should be sent only when your recipient is in an office and not picking up e-mail on a laptop. If the recipient cannot open your attachment on the laptop, it can lock him or her out of the computer.

11. Do not use ALL CAPS when writing in the body of your e-mail unless the CAPS are used for emphasis. Writing in ALL CAPS leaves the reader feeling as if you're screaming at them.

12. Use black as your font color. Avoid using colored text in business.

13. When replying back and forth to a person to gather or deliver information, you don't need to create an entirely new e-mail to your recipient each time. Instead, just hit reply to keep the thread alive for continuity references.

14. Anytime you mention a Web site, do your readers a favor and create the link in the body of your e-mail so they can click through to the site.

15. Do not forward chain letters or reply to spam from your office computer and *do not* surf areas on the Internet that are not work-related. Be forewarned, employees who surf the Internet and visit nonbusiness sites may be fired because of their habits. Some businesses have software that tracks such activities.

16. Use proper punctuation, capitalization, grammar, and spelling in e-mails. You have some room for casual writing but remain professional and don't take advantage of this style to avoid basic writing form all together. A generally agreed-on grievance is receiving e-mail from people who emulate the famous poet e.e. cummings (Edward Estlin Cummings) and use no capital letters.

17. Avoid using the e-mail function that requests a reply saying a person has read your e-mail.

18. Do not forward notices about viruses. If you're concerned about a virus you've heard about, forward a reliable news article on it to your system administrator. Invest in a virus protection program and update it often with the latest information.

19. Many people use e-mail to send jokes. Tell your friends not to send you jokes at the office, especially ones that are sexual in nature or target and demean any person or group based on gender, race, or ethnicity.

20. Smiley faces such as :-) are called emoticoms by those who enjoy chatting online and showing humor and emotion. They are commonly used in e-mails to save keystrokes or explanations. Use them sparingly and only with people you know. Choose only the most common ones to avoid confusing your reader. Some strange ones are circulating that only a handful of people understand; one example is **#8:]**, which is supposed to represent a smiling person who wears glasses and has a flat top. Would you know what that meant if you received it?

21. Begin an e-mail to a client with Dear So&So, followed by a colon. You may include Dr., Mr., Mrs., or Ms. before the last name. Address co-workers by their first names unless they are superiors; then it's best to use their formal title (Mr., Mrs.) before their last name.

22. Unlike telephone calls, you don't need to reply to all your e-mails. Some people receive hundreds a day and find it impossible to respond to them all. To save time, you can hit the reply button on those e-mails you intend to reply to later and delete those to which you will not reply. When you have a moment, work through your outbox and deal with them as quickly as possible.

Facts about Facsimiles

23. Include a cover sheet listing your company name, your name, the date, and the number of pages (including the cover sheet), as well as your fax and phone numbers.

24. Clearly state who the fax is meant for once it arrives at its destination. Many employees in offices and departments share a single fax machine. Don't assume your fax reaches the person's desk like an e-mail does. Keep a collection of pencils or broad-tipped markers by the fax machine to fill in the information on the cover sheet. These create a darker impression than a ballpoint pen.

25. Use a slightly larger and darker font than normal on your documents. Faxes with small print may transmit a blurry image and be difficult to read.

26. Avoid graphics that eat too much ink. Any graphic or logo that is too dark is thoughtless on the part of the sender.

27. There is a sense that faxes have a greater degree of urgency than e-mails. When you receive a fax, follow up in a timely manner.

28. Send faxes to home offices only during business hours to keep from waking everybody in the household at night.

29. Avoid sending faxes that are more than four pages. Lengthy documents tie up the receiver's machine and also use its ink. Try to mail anything larger than four pages.

Telephone and Voice-Mail Manners

30. When you answer your phone, state your name and, if appropriate, your department. For example, "Hello. Jim James, Human Resources."

31. Update your outgoing message daily to tell your caller your availability. Give a time when you will return a call or an extension to dial for another person who can help the caller. Do your best to route callers to an available person instead of dumping them into someone's voice mail. Your message might be, "Hello. This is Milton Brown. It's Wednesday, January 23, and I'm out of the office until 2:00 today, but I will return your call when I get back. If you need immediate assistance, press #489, and you will be directed to Steve White. Thank you."

> "Almost a third of Americans say talking on a cell phone in public is the 'rudest behavior' and women are more likely than men— 36 percent vs. 27 percent—to view cell phone talkers as rude."
>
> —*USA Today*, (10/01) International Communications Research for Southwest Airlines

32. If your call requires an interactive conversation and you want to avoid playing phone tag, leave a message that gives the best time(s) for the person to return your call.

33. Return your calls.

34. In case you have already forgotten number 33, return your calls.

35. Avoid screening your calls. It's poor business manners. However, if you're in an industry that receives unsolicited callers and you want to avoid them, dedicate one publicized number in your office to receive voice mails and

have another line that you give only to people you want to call you.

36. Listen more than you talk. Be considerate of other people's time. When you do speak, give concise information. Practice active-listening skills; ask questions and repeat the answers so your caller knows you're listening. For example, "You received the shipment on the 12th but not the invoices. Is that correct?"

37. At the end of a phone call, be direct with your caller and give your pertinent follow-up plans. For example, "I'll get back to you tomorrow by e-mail," or "I'll tell Jim you need those figures before the meeting." Finish with a sincere, "Good-bye."

38. Be brief when leaving a voice-mail message. Give your name, area code, and phone number slowly and carefully (spell your name if it is unusual) at the beginning of the message. This makes it easy for someone who did not catch your name and number to hit replay message and get the information right away.

39. If someone doesn't call you back immediately, don't leave subsequent messages unless your call is urgent.

40. When you call your voice-messaging center, be prepared with a pen and pad to record your calls. Note the date and day of the calls by recording them in a small notebook instead of on scrap paper or other business documents that might get filed or thrown away. By keeping the numbers all in one place, you can also refer to them in the future, if necessary. Make brief notes to jog your memory for follow-ups and tasks to add into your personal data organizer.

41. When you have time, look back over the notebook of your incoming calls and transfer the important phone numbers into your address book.

The Horrible Hold Button

42. Tell any caller you put on hold what you're doing and that you will be right back.

43. Be considerate of the person on hold and check back with the caller frequently to let her or him know where you are in your process. When you come back on the line, thank your caller for waiting.

44. If you're going to put the caller on hold for more than 60 to 90 seconds, ask your caller for his or her number and say you'll call back when you have the necessary information. If you need to take another call while someone is on the line with you, and you don't know how long the call will take, offer to call back when you're free or to put the person on hold.

45. Repeat the caller's name and number as a courtesy when you return to the line.

Tone, Diction, Timing, and Grammar on the Phone

46. Speak to your callers as if they were your only focus; do your best to center your mind and thoughts on them.

47. Speak clearly and slowly in full sentences and use excellent grammar.

48. Avoid saying, "yea," "uh huh," and "OK." Instead, say, "yes," "no," and "thank you."

49. Allow your speakers to finish their thoughts without interrupting.

50. Smile when you're on the phone. Your caller can hear you smiling.

Cell Phone Manners

51. A cell phone is no longer an indication of an individual's wealth, power, importance, or influence. Today, it is as common a convenience as a toaster. Just because you own a toaster doesn't mean that you need to have it with you at all times to toast bread. It's also best to turn it off during business meetings and social events. You may even choose to allow it to ring and gather messages while you're work-

ing, then pick up your messages when you take a break. Of course, there are times and occasions when you're expecting an important call. Then you can put your cell phone on the "vibrate mode" and tell your associates ahead of time that you're expecting an important call.

52. Find the instruction manual that came with your cell phone and refresh your memory on its functions regarding volume control, automatic dialing, and voice mail. Don't be the thoughtless bozo whose phone rings loudly in a business or social setting and then shrugs as if to say "Oops. I forgot to turn it off."

53. Don't walk into your office or anybody else's office while you're talking on a cell phone. Don't enter a restaurant, elevator, or reception area while chatting away as if you were a zombie oblivious to the world around you.

54. Leave your cell phone turned off (not on vibrate mode, but off) during funerals, classes, workshops, movies, theater and symphony performances, formal business meetings, meetings with your boss, a job interview, romantic moments, and other events. You don't want the cell to put the spotlight on you or take your attention away from the business (or pleasure) at hand.

55. Ten years ago, no one pulled out a cell phone during meals in a restaurant unless they were celebrities or top executives dining at Sardi's, The Pump Room, or The Polo Lounge. Now, everybody pulls their phones out for little or no reason. If you make or receive a call that's going to take more than a minute or two, excuse yourself from the table and find a place to talk that won't disturb the other guests at the restaurant. When you return, don't apologize or discuss the nature of the call but thank the people for allowing you to take it.

56. Don't scream into your cell phone. Its microphone is very sensitive and capable of transmitting your slightest whisper. Turn up the volume in your earpiece when you can't

hear people on the other end of the line. Suggest they turn up the volume in their earpiece in case they can't hear you.

57. Unless it's necessary that people have your cell phone number, don't print it on your business cards or leave it on your voice-mail message. Your cell phone is for your convenience and that of a select number of people. Give it only to those with a true need to reach you.

58. If you've left your number for someone to call you and they don't know it's for your cell phone, tell them when they reach you.

59. Remember that a cell phone call is just like your grandmother's party line; people are capable of listening in. Don't give away company secrets by thinking your calls are confidential because they're not.

60. Allow your voice mail to answer your calls when you're in heavy traffic or hazardous driving conditions.

61. Don't wear your listening earpiece or headset in your ear when not engaged in call. It is not a good fashion statement. Enough said. However, if you're driving, wear the earpiece for safety reasons if you're expecting a call.

62. Don't carry on conversations that other people can hear. One-sided conversations are considered a noise intrusion for bystanders.

63. In case you must have your cell phone turned on to create a sound instead of a vibration, please don't select musical tunes as your phone alert. It may amuse you, but most listeners are annoyed by your little tune.

Pager/Beeper Manners

64. Again, avoid the ring tone of your pager and keep it on the vibrate mode whenever possible.

65. It's OK to wait a moment to stop your beeper from vibrating when you're in the middle of an important conversation. When you do check your beeper, be discreet. Don't

throw your body around and make dramatic gestures that attract attention when you glance at your beeper.

|||||||||||||||||||||||||||||||||||||

CHAPTER SUMMARY

★ Technology can be a cold form of communication and is only meant to transmit data. Don't let it be a replacement for a face-to-face meeting.

★ E-mail is meant as a tool for sharing information. It is a communication device that has standards and modalities that should be followed. Please be aware of the constantly changing and shifting standards attributed to e-mail. This technology is evolving daily, and any rules that are set may be altered based on their use in the marketplace.

★ Faxes have a greater sense of urgency than e-mail; don't overuse them. Consider mailing any document longer than four pages.

★ A cell phone can be a rude intrusion to those not involved in a call. Use it in privacy but preferably not when driving. Use the vibrate mode of call announcement.

Client Protocol

B LOCKS OF UNINTERRUPTED TIME ARE considered a sacrosanct and precious commodity in today's business. People who grant you an appointment forfeit their time and focus on their own business concerns in order to spend time with you. They meet with you out of respect for you or your company, and because their time is so valuable, you should recognize and follow an aura of ritual in all business meetings.

People cannot absorb too much information at once, so get to the point when you're setting an appointment. Make your request in as few words as possible. Don't overtalk or beg for time. Be professional and brief.

Codes of Conduct for Setting an Appointment

When setting an appointment, state the following.

- Your name, your title, and your company's name.
  "This is Beth Bridges. I'm a sales representative with BCD Company . . ."

- How long you will need for the appointment.
  ". . . and I'd like to make an appointment with you for about an hour . . . "

- The reason you would like an appointment.
  ". . . to discuss the new features of our software."

- When you would like the appointment. Don't ask for permission. Remain respectful yet strong and direct.
  "Do you have some time this week after Wednesday? Or next week?"

You'll find out quickly whether or not giving contacts all the information they need to make a decision in two or three quick sentences is the right approach for securing your appointment. They may grant you an appointment with one of your suggested times, or they may may first ask you to mail them information that outlines the new features for your software and to call back

---

CASE STUDY 34

Making an Appointment

ISSUE

You want to book an appointment with one of your company's major clients in order to give the executive officer his company's productivity report for the year. What do you say to make the appointment?

SOLUTION

"Hello, this is Jose Rodriguez, account manager for FDG Company. I'd like to make an appointment with you for about an hour to go over your company's yearly productivity report. Is this Friday morning or next Wednesday afternoon available for us to get together?"

again to set up an appointment. Your suggested time is meant only to open the door for more discussions.

Codes of Conduct for Punctuality

American business requires punctuality. Be on time for all your appointments. However, when you have an appointment with a person outside your office, don't be surprised if you're asked to wait in a reception area for five to fifteen minutes while the person negotiates long halls, elevators, or escalators in order to greet you and take you back to his or her office. In case you are late, ask for forgiveness instead of saying "I'm sorry." Say, "Please forgive me for being late," and then continue your business. If you want to offer a brief explanation about why you're late, then do so. For example, "I was in a last-minute meeting."

> "Unfaithfulness in the keeping of an appointment is an act of clear dishonesty. You may as well borrow a person's money as his time."
>
> —HORACE MANN, CONSIDERED THE FATHER OF THE AMERICAN SCHOOL SYSTEM, 1796–1859

- When you're more than ten minutes early for an appointment, give the receptionist your business card and ask to wait to contact the person you're there to meet.
- When you're going to be less than ten minutes late because of traffic, call (if possible) and tell the receptionist or administrative assistant to the person you're meeting that you're detained in traffic, but you're on your way.
- In case you're going to be more than ten minutes late, call (if possible) and tell the receptionist, administrative

---

CASE STUDY 35

Punctuality Conduct

ISSUE

You're in a meeting with your boss, and you can see it's going to run overtime, causing you to miss a scheduled appointment. What do you do?

CASE STUDY 35, CONTINUED

SOLUTION

You excuse yourself from the meeting, call the administrative assistant for the person with whom you're meeting and reschedule your appointment for another time.

assistant, or person with whom you're meeting that you're detained. For example, "Please forgive me. I'm in a traffic jam and don't think I can make it to my appointment on time. Should I come to your office when the traffic breaks, or reschedule my appointment for another time?"

Codes of Conduct for Waiting Rooms

The next four Scenario Setups are specifically related to the protocol involved when you're calling on a client. In this series of checklists, imagine yourself to be J.K. Jones, a software representative. You're calling on Kim Kunes, head of accounting for Bittle and Broom Manufacturing Company, to explain the functions of the new accounting software Bittle and Broom has just purchased from your company. This section will teach you everything you need to know about

- waiting-room conduct,
- greeting your client and making rapport-building comments,
- getting to your point and concluding your meeting,
- codes of conduct for following up your meeting.

Scenario Setup: Waiting-Room Conduct

➤ Before you enter the lobby or reception area of Bittle and Broom, check your appearance and place two pristine business cards in a convenient place in your pocket or purse. Then upon entering, give one of the cards (upright with the type facing outward) to the receptionist and say, "Hello. I'm J.K. Jones, and I have an appointment with Kim Kunes at 10:00."

➢ In these days of heightened security, it is common for the receptionist to ask you to sign a visitor's book and wear a temporary badge on your jacket during the time you're on the company's premises.

➢ Decline any coffee the receptionist offers. Kim Kunes could arrive during the time the receptionist is pouring your coffee, and you don't want to have to carry the sloshing cup through the building to Kim's office or find a place to set down the coffee as you begin your appointment.

➢ After you have checked in with the receptionist, sit down and *do nothing.* Do not read the magazines. Do not make business calls or check your appointment book. Sit and wait *expectantly* for Kim to come into the lobby and take you to her office.

➢ When Kim enters the reception area, give her an eyebrow flash. (Remember, this is a small movement where the eyebrows are quickly raised and then lowered during a greeting. It gives the person you're greeting an unconscious message that you trust them. See Chapter 1.)

➢ As you give Kim your eyebrow flash, stand immediately and smile slowly. Accept her handshake if she offers it. If you've never met her before, hand her one of your business cards (right side up, type facing her). In case she doesn't offer a handshake, simply take her lead and follow her back to her office.

➢ Pay attention to the route to her office in case she doesn't have time to show you back to the lobby after your meeting. If you're the slightest bit nervous for your appointment, or her office is on the far side of a labyrinth of offices and cubicles, you may forget the route you originally took.

Scenario Setup: Greeting Your Appointment and Making Rapport-Deepening Comments

You are now inside Kim Kune's personal office.

➤ After you have followed Kim back to her office, wait to begin talking about business until you have reached her inner office area. She no doubt did her best to put you, the guest, at ease by telling you about the facility, asking about your drive, or making small talk.

➤ Once in Kim's office, she indicates where you should sit. In case she doesn't, ask her. After you've taken your seat, quietly open your briefcase, remove the paperwork you'll need for your meeting, and put your briefcase on the floor beside your chair.

➤ Kim offers you coffee, and you accept if you'd like some. Don't ask for coffee if she doesn't offer. Remember, time is money, and she wants you to conduct your business and leave immediately so she can get back to her own duties.

➤ At this point, your job is twofold: first, build rapport with Kim and second, present your information. Begin by thanking her for seeing you and then offer a small compliment or a kind comment to develop rapport. For example, "Nice view from your window," or "I know how busy you are and really appreciate you taking the time to see me," or "You've got quite an impressive collection of tennis trophies in your bookcase."

> "He speaks to me as if I was a public meeting."
> —Queen Victoria of Great Britain and Ireland, 1819–1901

➤ Next, launch into your purpose for being there. Move quickly from point to point without verbiage. Busy people have short attention spans.

➤ Now stop talking and invite Kim to talk by asking her questions and finding areas of agreement or commonality. Listen carefully and determine what she needs before you go further.

Scenario Setup: Getting to Your Point and Concluding Your Meeting

You're still in Kim's office. See how you get to the point of your meeting and then conclude your meeting.

> ➤ Kim is listening to you with more than her ears. She is unconsciously watching every move you make. Speak slowly and choose your words carefully. Smile. Maintain eye contact without staring her down and avoid glancing around the room. Allow your head to slowly rock back and forth in an affirmative movement that indicates "yes."

> ➤ Tell Kim Kunes why you're there. Be clear and direct in your comments. Keep that direct eye contact and say, "I'm here to show you the three new benefits of our software. Number one… "

> ➤ After you've given her the information, show her how to perform the functions of your software, hand her your color brochures, and ask if she has any questions. Once she understands the software, ask if she'd like you to meet with any of her people in accounting to educate them about its capabilities.

> ➤ Now that you have given Kim the information she needs, answered her questions, given her the tutorial CD and color brochures, and put any extra printed material back into your briefcase, then stand up. By being the one to stand and conclude the meeting, you show respect for Kim. This also puts you in control of the meeting. Thank her for her time, say good-bye, and mention that you will contact her again soon (in this case, in two weeks).

> ➤ Kim's correct business manners would be to show you back to the lobby and shake your hand good-bye there. However, she may offer to shake your hand in her office and ask you to see yourself out. In case you get lost (which

is easy to do in large maze-like offices), ask for directions from people in the hallway.

➤ Before you leave, sign out in the visitor's book and return your badge. Thank the receptionist and wish her or him a good day.

Scenario Setup: Following Up Your Meeting

Now, let's examine your codes of conduct for following up your meeting once you're back in your company office.

➤ As soon as you return to your office, send Kim a follow-up e-mail ping. In it say, "Thank you for taking the time to meet with me today. I hope I have answered your questions regarding the new functions of our software to your satisfaction. If I can be of further assistance to you, please do not hesitate to call me at 555-5230, extension, 219. I will call you in two weeks to set up an appointment to come in again and make sure your data transition has been made smoothly."

> "The man who removes a mountain begins by carrying away small stones."
> —WILLIAM FAULKNER, AMERICAN AUTHOR, 1897–1962

➤ Follow up your meeting and your e-mail with Kim at Bittle and Broom Manufacturing Company in two weeks. Good business relationships are based on excellent service, follow-up pings, and more follow-ups. (Depending on your industry, product, or service, you will need to know the timing necessary for your follow-up cycles with your client in order to stay in contact with them.)

|||||||||||||||||||||||||||||||||||||

CHAPTER SUMMARY

★ When setting appointments, be brief and offer enough information to open up the conversation for more dialogue.

★ If you're early, wait. If you're late, call.

★ When calling on a client outside the office, be punctual, deepen your rapport, get to the point, conclude your meeting, and follow up.

Choreographing the Business Dinner

|||||||||||||||||||||||||||||||||||||||||||||||||||||||||||||||

"It was a bold
man who first ate
an oyster."
—JONATHAN SWIFT, IRISH AUTHOR,
1667–1745

|||||||||||||||||||||||||||||||||||||||||||||||||||||||||||||||

N THIS ERA OF HIGH-TECH, LOW-TOUCH communication, the business meal is considered the quintessential opportunity for relationship building. Business dining in America is a highly evolved ritual created around a carefully orchestrated sequence of events and behaviors that involve sharing food, but underneath the clatter of knives, forks, and spoons is the palpable murmur of serious business at hand.

Please note that many business people (especially those from countries outside the United States) find the idea of mixing dining with business talk an extremely distasteful way to conduct business. They prefer talking about business during the workday and then relaxing and getting to know each other during meals. This section is for those circumstances in which

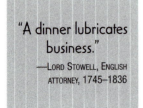

"A dinner lubricates business."

—Lord Stowell, English attorney, 1745–1836

business is *expected* to be conducted by all persons at the table during the dining experience.

There's much more to know about business dining than which utensil to use (although that's very important). Whether you're about to attend a final dinner interview with a prospective employer or dining with a prospective client, you need to know what's expected of you.

For questions about basic and formal table manners in America, please refer to some of the works on the reading list in the back of this book. This chapter focuses on the subtleties and nuances of creating the ideal conditions for entertaining an important client.

Scenario Setup: Fine Dining and Business

In the following scenario, you visit a five-star restaurant in a major American city that caters predominately to business people. You face normal circumstances that occur in an expensively priced American restaurant.

"Tell me what you eat and I will tell you who you are."

—Jean Anthelme Brillat-Savarin, famous gastronome and author of *The Physiology of Taste*, 1755–1826

You invite Sam Stone (a prospective client) to join you for a meal. During your time together, you do your best to sell yourself and your company to secure a $5 million contract. Sam is the CEO and final decision-maker involved in your negotiations and has the ultimate authority to award the account to you or grant it to your competitor.

This exercise may seem exaggerated, but it is not. The consummate professional plans every detail of business dining ahead of time to create a seamless scenario for conducting business. Nothing is left to chance. As you'll see, everything is carefully orchestrated to create a mutually beneficial outcome. You take Sam to dinner to enhance the probability that he will do business with you and your company.

> ➤ You call Sam Stone on the phone and invite him to join you for a meal. You ask if he has any restaurant preferences, and he says, "Anywhere you choose will be fine."

➤ You ask what time of day (breakfast, lunch, or dinner) he would like to meet you. You also ask if he has any specific time restraints or dietary needs as you make your restaurant choice. He tells you he has no dietary restrictions and agrees to join you for dinner next Tuesday at 7:00 P.M.

➤ Your company gives you the green light to take Sam to any restaurant of your choice. You choose The Bread and Grill Restaurant downtown. You call the restaurant and book a table for two for the following Tuesday at 7:00 P.M. (In case your company does not pay for your meal, choose a restaurant that's within your budget.)

➤ As you make the reservations, tell the person on the phone that this is an important business meal and request to be seated in a quiet area away from the kitchen and from any mirrors on the wall that might distrupt your conversation.

➤ Once you make the reservation, e-mail Sam the following information:
  • The name, address, and phone number for The Bread and Grill Restaurant,
  • the fact that reservation is in your name,
  • The time and date for your reservation.
  • Your office and cell phone number in case he needs to reach you. (If you don't have a cell phone, or if it's a breakfast meeting, include your home phone number.)

➤ The day before your planned dinner with Sam, e-mail him to say you're looking forward to seeing him the next evening at 7:00 P.M. at the Bread and Grill Restaurant on the corner of Clark and Grand.

➤ On Tuesday evening, you arrive at the Bread and Grill Restaurant a few minutes early to officially greet Sam. The first thing you do is turn your cell phone off completely. You wait at the entrance of the restaurant instead of being seated at the table. Or you may be seated at your table and wait for him there. If you've never met Sam and want to plan ahead, ask the maitre d' to bring him to the table and formally introduce you. Tip the maitre d' ahead of time for this extra attention by shaking his hand with money in your palm. Don't touch anything on the table while you wait, or pick up a napkin, or take a drink of water.

➤ When Sam arrives, shake his hand and say hello. The maitre d' takes you to your table. Along the way you notice Sam's watch is on his left hand. You assume he is right-handed.

➤ The maitre d' leads you to a square table, and you motion for Sam to sit on your right with his back to the wall (the power position). Anyone on your right is considered an honored guest. However, if Sam is left-handed, seat him on your left (with his back to the wall) so he doesn't feel crowded. In this way you take *charge* of your table and demonstrate to Sam that he is your guest for the evening.

➤ After you are seated, the maitre d' hands you each a menu and leaves the wine list on the table.

➤ If Sam were a female executive, she would pull out her own chair and push herself up to the table without assistance as a man would; however, it is still polite for a gentleman to lightly touch the back of a lady's chair as she seats herself. That is all that is necessary to show your respect. If you believe a woman might not like this gesture, listen to your instincts and don't do it. Women never touch the back of each other's chairs regardless of their rank or title.

➤ You meet your server for the evening, speak quietly and respectfully, and ask him or her to watch for your signal for attention but not to interrupt any conversation at the table.

➤ Sam orders a glass of the house's white wine, and so do you. Don't drink too much, even if Sam does. You don't order an alcoholic beverage unless he does. If Sam orders a glass of wine and you're a nondrinker (or not in the mood), don't feel obligated to join him. In case he wants to order a bottle of wine and you're not drinking, say, "I'm not joining you tonight, but please, order a bottle anyway." You may quietly ask your server to remove your wine glass if there's already one on the table. There's no need to apologize or offer excuses for not drinking. Just say to Sam, "I prefer iced tea (or iced water or whatever you're drinking)." Since many people are nondrinkers today, chances are he'll understand.

➤ You and Sam begin to make small talk. This is the thing for a gracious host/hostess to do. (Remember the rules for small talk: at a breakfast meeting, wait to discuss business until you've both been given your coffee; at a luncheon, practice small talk until you've both ordered; at dinner, make small talk for the first 30 minutes of the evening.)

➤ Whether you're male or female, you are responsible for your guest. When Sam's water glass is low, signal your server that he needs more water. It's your responsibility to be attentive to his needs.

➤ The headwaiter comes to your table to take your order. You defer to Sam to order first from the menu. (In many fine restaurants, a headwaiter takes your order but does not deliver your food.) This is when the headwaiter tells you the restaurant's specials for the evening.

➤ Sam asks you for menu suggestions, but because you've never been to this restaurant before, you ask the headwaiter for a recommendation.

➤ Sam orders an appetizer, and so do you. You don't order one unless he does. After dinner, he orders a dessert, and so do you. You don't order a dessert unless he does.

➤ Order something easy to eat; avoid ordering spaghetti, lobster or crab legs, or anything that requires a bib or must be forced open with tongs.

➤ Speak to your server often during the meal to let her or him know you are the *point person* at the table. Always thank the server quietly each time service is offered.

➤ Use the time between ordering your meal and your food's arrival to slowly begin discussing business matters. Sam knows why you're having dinner together, and chances are he'll be waiting for you to broach the subject. Begin your business discussion with some sincere flattery about the people you've been dealing with in his company by saying, "I've really enjoyed working with Jill Jacobs and Bret Brown." Compliment him on the company or the product or service his company offers by saying, "Your company has created such a value to your customers." You don't need to lie or drip with sentiment, but say *something* that demonstrates your interest.

➢ When the soup, salad, or appetizer arrives, begin to speak more in-depth about your business.

➢ As you begin to eat, ask Sam if he has everything he needs. If not, motion to your server and speak on Sam's behalf.

➢ Unfortunately, when Sam's food arrives, it hasn't been properly prepared. You signal your server who takes his dish back to the kitchen. You stop eating until Sam's food has been fixed in the kitchen and redelivered to him.

➢ As the dinner progresses through the entree, be aware that Sam has had a long day and will be more amenable, relaxed, and receptive 15 minutes after he has begun eating. This should give you another half hour to talk about business before his blood rushes to his stomach, the digestion process begins, and he begins to get tired.

➢ When he's finished eating and relaxed, *tell* Sam you'd like to conduct business with him and his company. It's far better to tell him you'd like to do business with him than to ask him if he wants to do business with you. For example, "Sam, it would be an honor to do business with you and your company. Do you have any specific questions I can answer for you at this time?"

➢ This is a pivotal moment. You must wait for Sam's response without saying a word or moving a muscle. Maintain direct eye contact with Sam. The next 30 seconds will give you direction for your next moves.

➢ Hopefully, Sam will tell you he wants to do business with you in his first comment. If so, thank him for his confidence and assure him you'll deliver a quality product or service. If he doesn't immediately say he wants to do business in his first comment, it means he has lingering doubts about giving you his business, and he will move directly to questions he needs answered to his satisfaction before moving further with negotiations.

➤ If Sam has questions at this time, he may (hopefully) order dessert or coffee after dinner and remain attentive and want to talk further about business. Without dessert or coffee, he may quiet down, and you should plan to leave before his attention lags and he begins thinking about the rest of his evening, or (worse yet) he gets sleepy. You want Sam to leave the restaurant feeling positive about your time together, not dull and tired. So don't linger a moment longer than necessary once the food has been cleared from the table. Leave right away. Any further business conversations can be continued at a later time.

➤ Ask the server to give the check to you. Always avoid fighting for it. To make sure you pay for the meal and avoid any awkward discussions, tell Sam he has been your honored guest for the evening. If you're concerned that Sam may insist on buying the meal, ask your server or the maitre d' when you first arrive at the restaurant to imprint your credit card, then add a tip, sign it and get the server to bring you a receipt at the end of the meal.

➤ Tip your server 20 percent of your pretax check. (The word tip is an acronym for **T**o **I**nsure **P**romptitude.) In certain parts of the country, it has become a popular trend to discreetly tip servers prior to your meal the amount you would normally leave to insure promptitude and extraordinary service.

➤ In this case, you tipped the maitre d' earlier in the evening for seating you, but you could also tip him at the end of the evening when you tip the headwaiter. You never need to offer extra tips to the headwaiter, maitre d', or wine steward unless the service has gone beyond your expectations; the amount of any tip is up to you. In some formal restaurants in major cities, the headwaiter, maitre d', and sommelier (wine steward) enjoy extravagant tips (delivered in a handshake) ranging from $5 to $50 or more for each visit. A tip for a wine steward is generally around $5 per bottle opened or 15 percent to 20 percent of the pretax cost of the wine. In this case, you tipped the headwaiter (who took your order) 5 percent of the pretax cost of your meal and tipped the maitre d' $10 for seating you at a quiet table.

➤ You tip the person in the coat room $1 per item for taking Sam's overcoat.

➤ You also offer to pay for Sam's valet parking if the restaurant doesn't validate it.

➤ This is another critical moment during your evening with Sam. While you're walking to the front of the restaurant, tell Sam how you will follow up with him. For example, "I'll call you on Thursday to discuss signing the contract," or "Tomorrow, I'll e-mail you information to help you make your decision."

➤ Offer to shake hands and thank Sam for joining you.

➤ The next day, send Sam a note telling him you enjoyed spending time with him and look forward to doing business together.

➤ Contact Sam again when you said you would.

Scenario Setup: When You're Someone's Guest at a Restaurant

Now, reverse the role. This time, you are the guest of someone who wants to ask for your business. You also have certain responsibilities to your host.

➤ Someone asks you to join her or him for a meal and you are courteous enough to get back to the invitation quickly.

➤ You provide your host or hostess with the information needed to make plans for your time together. For example, the date and time you can meet or any dietary restrictions you may have. Avoid suggesting a specific restaurant because it may not be in your contact's budget.

➤ In case your host or hostess does not confirm your appointment the day prior to the meal, call to say you're looking forward to meeting the following day at the appointed time and location.

> "For let me tell you, that the more the pleasures of the body fade away, the greater to me is the pleasure and charm of conversation."
>
> —PLATO, *THE REPUBLIC*, GREEK PHILOSOPHER, 427–347 B.C.

➤ Order moderately priced selections of food and wine, since you don't know budgetary parameters. If your host or hostess wants to order an expensive bottle of wine, then it's clearly within his or her budget to do so.

➤ Don't feel pressured to drink alcohol. Again, it's perfectly acceptable to just say no without offering any apology or excuse.

➤ Be punctual. In case you're running late, call your host or hostess or the restaurant to say you're on your way.

➤ Do your best to be pleasant and personable during the meal. Practice the 30-Day Rule and make a respectful amount of obligatory small talk.

➤ Thank your hostess or host after the meal by calling, e-mailing, or dropping a note in the postal mail. Make some gesture to acknowledge his or her generosity for inviting you to a meal.

✔ Checklist: Dressing for Dinner

❑ You need to know the dress code, so you call the restaurant or your host and ask if it's necessary for you to dress in evening attire (coat, tie, cocktail-level dressing). It's always better to overdress a bit in business situations than to underdress.

❑ When weather requires that you wear an overcoat or raingear and you're dining in a formal restaurant, arrive a minute or two early to check your coat or umbrella in the coat room. Leave your hat or cap in the coat room instead of taking it to the table with you.

||||||||||||||||||||||||||||||||||

CHAPTER SUMMARY

★ Successful business meals are planned to the smallest detail to assure their success.

★ When you are the host or hostess for a business meal, you are responsible for your guest's needs and comfort.

★ When your guests drink a beverage with alcohol, you may join them and drink also. Don't drink when they don't. Never feel like you must join them or offer apologies or excuses when you're a nondrinker.

★ Always check ahead to determine dress codes at restaurants.

Gift Giving, Conventions, Events, and Social Occasions

I
N THE COURSE OF CONDUCTING BUSINESS and improving your client relations, you will encounter many social opportunities for you to demonstrate the quality of your character and ethics. Social events, from the convention dinner to the company barbeque, call for you to lighten up, and in this chapter, you'll learn how to do that without compromising your professionalism. Gift giving is an integral part of many social occasions. You can show your clients and employer consideration and maintain company morale by choosing and properly delivering an appropriate gift.

> "If a man insisted always on being serious, and never allowed himself a bit of fun and relaxation, he would go mad or become unstable without knowing it."
>
> —HERODOTUS, GREEK HISTORIAN, 484–420 B.C.

Business Gift Giving

There are several excellent reasons for gift giving:

- To offer thanks to a new client for the decision to hire your company's services or buy it's products.
- When you want to show your appreciation to an associate for a job well done.
- To show your support for a wedding, the birth of a child, a retirement, or an associate's anniversary.
- To show your condolences when a business associate loses a family member or to offer support when someone has been hurt or is ill.
- As a gesture of thanks or outstanding service.
- To congratulate special people on their birthdays. Birthdays are not usually celebrated in offices unless there's a departmental celebration (a cake and public mention) each month. Even then, gifts and cards are not required unless you have a special relationship with the person and want to give a gift.
- When someone in your company is promoted or has excelled in some special area. Perhaps she or he graduated from a certification program, closed a large account, or created a pertinent program related to your company's effectiveness.

Before giving or receiving a business gift, ask someone in the human resource division about your company's gift-giving policies. Many companies now have policies stating that employees may not accept gifts from outsiders. Other companies have more relaxed gift policies but may have clear cost guidelines and restrictions. For example, they may require that consumable gifts (food or candy) be under $25.

Seven Things to Know about Business Gift Giving

Here are some suggestions to help guide you through your gift giving.

1. Give well-thought-out and meaningful gifts. There is one major guideline for business gift giving: "Give a gift the person would enjoy receiving." In other words, do your homework to learn something about the person that gives you an idea for a business gift; the more you personalize the gift, the more appropriate the gift is. For example, you might give someone who plays golf a nicely wrapped box of golf balls with his or her name or initials printed on them. A cook might enjoy a chef's apron with the company logo embroidered on the front. And a gardener might like a nice pair of gardening gloves or a trowel with his or her name engraved.

2. Senior executives often send senior executives at other companies larger business gifts (more than $200). There are professional corporate gift consultants at major retail stores (Tiffany & Co., Nordstroms, Saks Fifth Avenue, Neiman Marcus, Bloomingdale's) who can help you find the perfect gift.

3. If your company is considering giving a very expensive gift (more than $500) such as travel, a painting, portrait, or sculpture to a client-company or customer, contact a professional in that field to help you decide on a gift.

4. Be sensitive to the subtleties and symbolism of gift giving for people from various cultures. For example, never give a clock as a gift to a Chinese associate in America since the words *death* and *clock* are similar. It would be a double insult to wrap the clock to your Chinese associate in white paper, since the color white in Chinese culture represents bad luck.

5. Whether you're giving a small token gift or a large one, it's important that it be wrapped and accompanied by an appropriate and personally signed card. It's also good manners to include a business card so the recipient will have your name and street address and can write you a thank-you note.

6. Try to personally hand your gift to the recipient; however it's not necessary for the person to open it right then. It's

also acceptable to send a gift in the mail as long as you place it in another box to protect the wrapping.

7. Avoid giving religious gifts or cards during the Christmas season to those who are not Christians by faith. Instead, opt for a card that wishes them a happy holiday or happy new year.

How Much to Spend

- Token gifts under $25 can be given to thank people for their business. However, if your company considers this gift a thank-you for a big account, then the value of the gift may vary according to the size of the account and range from $500 to $2,000.

- A standard amount to spend on a gift for a person in senior management is $50.

- The standard amount to spend on a gift for a person in lower to midlevel management is $10 to $25.

- You should spend $25 to $50 on a gift to your administrative assistant (depending on how long the person has been with you and the company). It's also acceptable to give cash to an administrative assistant. Make sure you include a personally signed card.

- Those in senior management (who have more income) often give lavish gifts ranging from $200 to $2,000 to other senior executives.

What to Give

- To make your gift personal, consider what your recipient enjoys. If your client loves a good cigar, then one or two would make an ideal business gift, especially if they're his favorite brand. If your client is a woman and loves shopping at a particular department store, give her a gift certificate from that store.

- Perishable items are good business gifts. For example, food baskets, chocolates, wine, champagne, brandy, soaps, flowers (not red roses), plants, perfumes, or aftershave (if you're sure it's the fragrance they use).

- You might choose office décor, such as a leather desk blotter case, elegant letter opener, glass paperweight, frame for a photograph or diploma, or a set of bookends.
- For someone who enjoys music, CDs or tickets to the symphony or a concert (make sure the recipient enjoys that musical genre) make good gifts.

Office Party Etiquette

When you attend a business-related party outside your normal working hours, there's an implied assumption by your employer that you will maintain a high level of business acumen. People who let down their guard at the annual company party and act unprofessionally by drinking too much and making inappropriate comments nearly always regret their behavior the next day. This section encourages you to relax and enjoy yourself at business-related social events yet remember that your behavior is on display and that professional attitudes and behaviors are expected. Lose sight of this fact and you could pay the consequences.

> "When you play, play hard; when you work, don't play at all."
>
> —THEODORE ROOSEVELT, 26TH PRESIDENT OF THE U.S., 1858–1919

RSVP

The letters RSVP stand for the French phrase *répondez, s'il vous plait* which means please reply. Americans are lax about promptly responding to social invitations; however, it's not good manners to keep a host or hostess in the dark about whether you'll be accepting or declining. When you receive an invitation to a social event that is business related, reply with professional promptness. Some invitations request a reply only when you're expressing your regrets for not being able to attend. Follow the host or hostess guidelines for replying. If the party invitation invites you to bring a guest, and you plan to, let your host or hostess know ahead of time.

Buffets, Barbeques, and Pool Parties

> "My best friend is the one who brings out the best in me!"
>
> —Henry Ford, creator of Ford Motor Company, 1863–1947

Just because a business gathering of associates is in a casual setting doesn't mean you can let your hair down and act like a clown. In order to be included and invited back to social events, set your standards high.

The more business-related affairs you attend, the more comfortable you'll begin to feel. For example, it takes practice to learn how to maneuver your way through a buffet line while talking about business and juggling a beverage; but the more you do it, the easier it becomes. Well, maybe it never becomes *easy*, but you can learn to balance your plate and eat at the same time. Never forget the main reason you attend business-related social events: to make contacts and maintain the business ones you already have for the good of your company. Yes, you're there to enjoy yourself and have fun, but more importantly, you're there out of professional courtesy.

Scenario Setup: Attending Buffets, Barbeques, and Pool Parties

For this exercise, imagine you've been invited to a Fourth of July swimming party held at your boss' home, in his backyard. There is a lavish buffet of various foods, including barbeque ribs dripping with sauce. There are 50 people attending the party; ten are from your office, 20 are friends of your boss and his wife, and 20 are potential clients for your company.

> ➤ When you arrive at the party, you and your guest (your spouse or a friend) find your boss and his wife and thank them for inviting you. Do this again before you leave. To practice extra good manners, send a handwritten thank-you note to your host and hostess that will arrive in the mail within a week after the party; when you see your boss at work, give him a flattering comment and say, "Thanks for inviting us. It was a great buffet," or "We had a nice time. You have a terrific pool."

➤ Since the party is in a private home, you and your spouse take a small token gift to your host and hostess. This gesture shows your appreciation for their hospitality. In this case, you and your spouse have brought your boss and his wife two chocolate truffles wrapped in tissue and a ribbon. It's a small gift, but the thought and the gesture are what counts.

➤ You use your time in line at the buffet or bar to introduce yourself and your spouse to people around you. You create casual conversations and look for ways to inject information about your company. Although it's a party and you're not there to do business and sell your company or its products or services, you are there out of professional courtesy and should always be a good representative of your company.

➤ Both you and your spouse place small amounts of food on your plates instead of piling them too high. It's fine to return for more. Every time you pass through the buffet line, you take that opportunity to speak to new people. You make it a point to appear relaxed and engaged with others in conversation.

> "Business is like riding a bicycle. Either you keep moving or you fall down."
> —Frank Lloyd Wright, American architect, 1869–1959

➤ You and your spouse do not pick up food in the buffet line and pop it into your mouths. Instead, you each choose the items you want to eat, then use a fork or utensil to put them on your plate. Put them in your mouth after you've left the buffet line.

➤ When a server passes hot appetizers, you select one, and place it on your plate or on a napkin before putting it in your mouth. You are careful not to select an appetizer from the server's tray and place it directly into your mouth.

➤ Since it's a juggling act to hold a small food plate and a drink and still be able to feed yourself without spilling, you set your drink down on a coaster until you've finished eating.

➤ Thank the server each time she or he offers you an appetizer or a drink.

➤ You are careful not to talk with your mouth full. When you are eating, you let others talk, and you nod frequently and smile to let them know you are listening.

➤ After eating a sticky barbeque, you excuse yourself, find a washroom, and clean your hands.

➤ People are beginning to swim after lunch. You're not required to swim at a pool party, but you and your spouse want to take a dip. You've each brought swimsuit, pool sandals, and towel. It's an afternoon party, so you've also brought your own sunscreen and hat.

➤ You each have one margarita and both of you stay sober. You are clearly aware that business-related social events are a time for business, not out-of-control drinking.

✔ Checklist: Planning for a Business Conference, Convention, or Banquet

When planning to attend a conference, try to take the following steps ahead of time.

❑ Study your convention guide before you leave home and know what you want for an outcome.

❑ Sign up to attend specific workshops or hear speakers.

❑ Reserve your seats for dinners or keynote speaker banquets.

❑ Call people you know will also be attending and schedule time with them.

❑ Know who you want to talk to during the convention and what you want to accomplish with them.

❑ Decide where you want to spend your time.

❑ Decide how you want to use your resources. For example, decide how many samples of your product or brochure you will need, how much money you need, and how you plan to schedule your time and energy.

❑ Plan your extracurricular activities ahead of time by making dinner reservations at local restaurants, booking tours, and special events.

❑ Take plenty of business cards.
❑ Make sure you take at least two pairs of comfortable shoes.

Those who attend conventions, conferences, and banquets spend much of their daytime hours talking about business. When evening comes and attendees are far from home, they tend to unwind and relax just as they would on a vacation. It's important to plan ahead for your convention experience, or you may exhaust yourself and get little done by keeping late hours and then trying to work all day.

Scenario Setup: Attending a Conference Banquet

Convention banquets are a time for the majority of participants to join together in a large hotel ballroom to have a meal, listen to a keynote speaker, and learn about the awards of those in your field who have excelled. The following are some suggestions for joining a party of ten at a round banquet table.

➤ Try not to sit with someone you know. Use your banquet as a time to meet new people and make contacts. After all, if you are seated at a table with nine people you work with every day, you won't be able to network at the event.

➤ When given the choice of where to sit, wait until the tables begin to fill up before choosing a table to join. By sitting down too early, you may end up next to people you're not interested in meeting.

➤ Unless you have been assigned a specific table, sit with people you would like to meet or to introduce to each other.

➤ Round tables that seat eight or ten people are complicated because of all the utensils, plates, napkins, coffee cups, and glasses. They are generally a formula for disaster when people are trying to decide whose table setting belongs to whom. Have a sense of humor about this problem and do your best to find what's yours.

➤ Picking up the wrong napkin at a round table of ten can create a domino effect. It happens often when creative waiters place ornately folded napkins in wine or water glasses (at the head of your knife) and coffee cups (to the right of your knife and spoon). Your napkin is generally the one next to (or under) your forks to the left of your plate. If someone at your table gets shorted a napkin, use the confusion as an icebreaker, and after a moment of levity, give the person the leftover one.

➤ When the person next to you uses the wrong bread and butter plate (which is slightly to the left above your forks), then you end up without one and someone else gets two. In this case, it is best to say nothing and use your dinner plate for bread and butter to keep from embarrassing the person who is now using your plate.

➤ When the keynote speaker or awards banquet ceremony begins and your back is to the front of the room, turn your chair around. You'll have your back to those at your table, but that's considered appropriate under banquet circumstances.

➤ Don't talk and whisper at your table when people are speaking at the microphone. If your conversation is important, take it out of the room and come back when you're finished.

➤ Turn the ringer on your cell phone to the vibrating mode before the banquet. If you receive a call during the keynote address, please don't answer it and then walk out of the banquet hall with the phone at your ear to make yourself look important. It's rude to the keynote speaker and to everyone in the room to draw attention away this way. Besides that, you look like a bozo.

➤ Tell your server to remove your glass when you're not drinking wine.

➤ It's acceptable to ask your server for iced tea, hot tea or coffee, but wait until everyone at your table has been served their entree.

➤ You may ask your server to adjust your meal preparation if it's not to your liking, but wait until everyone at your table has been served.

➤ Don't take home the centerpiece after the banquet unless someone at the microphone invites guests to do so.

Scenario Setup: Being an Invited Guest at a Business Associate's Wedding

It's an honor to receive an invitation to a work associate's wedding. After all, the bride and groom and their families are spending a large amount of money and time to put on a spectacular gala, and you're invited to attend and enjoy yourself. You are also charged with maintaining a professional demeanor during every aspect of the festivities. Don't expect to be able to relax and enjoy yourself the way you might at your cousin Burt's wedding while at the wedding for you boss' son; it's a mistake to think you can maintain the same level of behavior at both events.

> "Love is faith, and one faith leads to another."
> —HENRI-FRÉDÉRIC AMIEL, SWISS PHILOSOPHER AND POET, 1821–1881

Imagine you received an invitation to attend the wedding of Maria Johnson, who is an associate of yours in the office. She is marrying Eric Brown on a Saturday afternoon at a local country club. You responded as quickly as possible and accepted her gracious offer to attend her wedding festivities. She also invited you to bring a guest, and you've asked Brenda Bueller to accompany you. You know only a few people from your office who are also attending, and it may not be a terribly exciting event, but you decide to be the perfect guest. You attend with the idea that yes, you're there to enjoy yourself, but more importantly, to show collegial support to your business associate and her new husband on their happy day.

➤ You are punctual for the wedding. A few of your business associates were not invited to the ceremony but only to the following dinner and reception. You and your guest were invited to both.

➤ You realize that bringing a date to a wedding is an additional responsibility for you. You introduce Brenda Bueller to your business associates and other wedding guests you speak with during the afternoon. When you have the chance, you introduce her to the bride and groom, and she thanks them for the opportunity to attend their wedding.

➤ Since Brenda doesn't know anyone except you, you make the effort to include her in conversations. It often seems as if everyone knows each other at wedding festivities, and strangers can feel left out of the fun if they're not included.

➤ One of your office associates was invited but could not attend, so she sent a small gift and a card to show her support.

➤ The invitation announced that the dress code for the Saturday afternoon wedding was *cocktail dress*, so you wear a dark suit, and Brenda wears a conservative dress. No women in the room wear white or cocktail clothes that might outshine the beauty of the bride on her special day.

➤ A few people in your office contributed to a small fund and collectively bought a wedding gift for the bride and groom. They all put their names on the wedding card. It's not an extravagant gift, but it was ordered from the place the couple registered for their wedding gifts, and you contributed a few dollars. Some people in your office signed a card to send to the bride and groom instead of contributing to a gift.

➤ After the nuptials, you and Brenda stand in the receiving line to shake hands with the bride and groom. To the bride you say, "Best wishes." To the groom, you say, "Congratulations." It is improper to congratulate a bride for finding a husband.

➤ After the wedding, you're invited to a seated meal. You don't know anyone at your table, so you introduce yourself and Brenda to everyone and act as pleasant dinner guests.

➤ The close friends of the bride and groom make zany, funny, and off-color wedding toasts, but as a business associate, you don't. After the family, groomsmen, and bridesmaids finish their toasts, it's time for the guests to offer one. You've come prepared with a simple toast that is kind and supportive. You rise from your chair, lift your glass in the direction of the bride and groom, and say, "May your marriage be one of enduring happiness and joy. I salute you," and you take a small sip from your glass. After your toast, you sit down.

➤ If you had gone to the wedding alone, you would have used this time to socialize and make new friends and contacts. An ideal way to create rapport with strangers at a wedding is to talk to them about their relationship with the bride and groom. Ask questions such as "How do you know the bride and groom?"

➤ You've thought ahead and taken business cards to the wedding. You meet a man you enjoyed talking with or want to see again, so you exchange cards with him.

CHAPTER SUMMARY

★ Give a gift someone would like to receive to commemorate a specific event.

★ Check gift-giving and gift-receiving policies within companies to comply with their standards.

★ When you're invited to a social event in someone's home, promptly RSVP. Take a small token gift, greet your host and hostess when you arrive, thank them when you leave, and maintain a professional demeanor. Send a thank-you note.

★ Plan ahead before attending a business conference so that, you can make good use of your time while you're there.

★ When you're invited to a business associate's wedding, use your highest level of manners throughout the event.

DIVERSITY AND DISABILITY IN THE WORKPLACE

Diversity in the
Workplace

N EWSFLASH: IT'S A SIGN OF STRENGTH and wisdom to celebrate the differences in all people and treat everyone with respect and sensitivity. If you have a personal bias toward any group of people, it's *your* responsibility to adjust your attitudes and behaviors. Failure to take personal responsibility for your bigotry can cause legal problems for your company, high employee turnover, and low office morale.

Melissa Balaban,[1] an attorney specializing in human resource solutions, offers a valuable suggestion for teaching workplace diversity. She suggests employers create respectful

---

[1] Melissa Balaban, Esq., senior consultant, Employment Practices Solutions, (800) 727-2766, mbalaban@epexperts.com.

work environments that establish safe places for their employees to feel good about where they work and not just because they want to avoid lawsuits. Ms. Balaban says, "The new golden rule in relation to the workplace is, 'Do unto others as *they* would like to be treated.' Diversity inspires creativity and success in America today. Employers and employees both need to approach problems in a new and different way than ever before to solve problems in the most effective ways possible; that is what diversity is all about!"

For more information about diversity in the workplace, please refer to the reading list in the back of this book.

Religious Sensitivity in the Workplace

"If we are to achieve a richer culture, rich in contrasting values, we must recognize the whole gamut of human potentialities, and so weave a less arbitrary social fabric, one in which each diverse human gift will find a fitting place."

—MARGARET MEAD, ANTHROPOL-OGIST, AUTHOR, LECTURER, AND SOCIAL CRITIC, 1901–1978

There is an immediate need for instruction regarding religious sensitivity in the workplace. According to Georgette Bennett, Ph.D., president of The Tanenbaum Center for Interreligious Understanding in New York City,[2] "Religious bias may be inadvertent in the workplace environment, but it does exist. It's a product of ignorance because Americans know so little about each other's religion. According to 66 percent of those surveyed reported "…religious bias exists in their workplace." Out of the 66 percent, 20 percent said they had experienced it directly or knew of someone in the workplace who had. These were not one-time experiences, but episodes that occurred several times a month."

Dr. Bennett goes on to say, "The greatest antidote to ignorance and bigotry is contact and communication. It's important for all people to have the opportunity to talk to each other and learn from each other in order to create

***

[2] The Tanenbaum Center for Interreligious Understanding in New York City, (212) 967-7707, www.tanenbaum.org.

a safe space…. It's important to be aware that it's the 'small stuff' that can harm people and make them feel excluded and feel like second-class citizens."

✔ Checklist: Respect for Others' Religions

❑ Be respectful when an associate celebrates a religious holiday you don't know about or understand. Ask about the holiday and how its significance is celebrated.

❑ Show respect to an associate who prays or meditates at a certain time or location during a business day.

❑ Respect people of faiths other than Christian when you're at an office Christmas party by wishing them a "Happy Holiday" rather than "Merry Christmas."

❑ Choose a variety of food when planning an office Christmas party where there will be people of various faiths to accommodate those who eat only vegetarian or kosher food.

❑ When planning an office party where there will be people from various cultures and faiths, don't play only religious Christian music such as "Away in a Manger" or "Oh Holy Night." Instead, choose nonreligious holiday standards such as "Let It Snow" and "Winter Wonderland."

> "We are in a fight for our principles, and our first responsibility is to live by them. No one should be singled out for unfair treatment or unkind words because of their ethnic background or religious faith."
>
> —PRESIDENT GEORGE W. BUSH, SEPTEMBER 20, 2001

Gender Sensitivity Toward Women in the Workplace

Women are finding their way to the top of the corporate ladder. Slowly. Very slowly. According to Linda Wirth,[3] a senior gender specialist for the International Labor Organization's Bureau for

---

[3] Linda Wirth, author of report for International Labor Organization's (ILO) Bureau for Gender equality titled "Breaking Through the Glass Ceiling: Women in Management."

Gender Equality, women now hold executive management positions in 5.1 percent of America's largest 500 companies. Women have found their way to the position of trusted first lieutenants in the top order of the executive ranks. Now, to become captains of the ship, they need to practice and rehearse strong "lead-her-ship" skills.

Colle Davis,[4] CEO of Executive Mentoring and Coaching Inc. in Beverly Hills, California, works with many top executives in corporate America. He says, "Women represent the largest untapped resource that companies have. By empowering and promoting women within their company, they will directly add to their bottom line. America's predominately male executive leadership needs to wake up and acknowledge the skills, talents, and abilities of their female workforce by grooming and promoting more women to the top level of executive. It's a brave new world, and men and women should both be leading it."

In order for women to rise to levels of leadership, they must continue to refine their skills and step forth toward solutions with conviction and a strong voice filled with self-confidence to create loyalty in their troops. First, however, a radical behavioral shift needs to occur in the minds and attitudes of America's leadership and workforce to grant women their right to be strong, self-promoting, and to speak without fear of censure and being called that "B" word behind their back.

✔ Checklist: Respect for the Businesswoman

❑ Allow a woman to finish speaking and don't talk over or interrupt her when she challenges an issue or person (or group of people) with a valid point. She should not have to resort to raising her voice and be thought of as a screamer. When she's finished talking, then you can have your turn.

---

[4] Colle Davis, CEO, Executive Mentoring and Coaching Inc. 9663 Santa Monica Blvd., Beverly Hills, CA 90210, www.mycoach.com.

❑ Offer women the respect and courtesy of listening to them when they speak openly about their personal successes in the workplace. Congratulate them when they finish instead of judging them or talking about your own successes.

❑ Listen to a woman's recommendations when she offers a solution to a problem. Respond to her in a timely manner whether you take her suggestions or not.

❑ Treat women leaders in your office with the same respect you would male leaders. Don't attempt to offer them excuses for your work in hopes of appealing to their feminine nature.

❑ Listen carefully to a woman's comments during a business meeting and respond with the same respect you would if a man were speaking. In fact, make an effort to encourage women to speak up and be heard in meetings.

❑ Allow women privacy regarding their marital status. If they want you to know personal information, they'll volunteer it.

Ethnic Sensitivity in the Workplace

All people are called upon to practice patience, tolerance, and inclusion in the workplace. America is filled with people from every corner of the world. It shouldn't be up to company policy to mandate that employees show respect for one another; all of us should make that decision for ourselves. However, the growing influx of immigrants over the past few decades and recent political turmoil have made it necessary to readdress the issue of ethnic sensitivity in the workplace.

Billy E. Vaughn, Ph.D.,[5] president and founder of The Diversity Training University International LLC, offers companies diversity and cross-cultural training programs. "We work within companies to teach people the impact their behavior has when they're dealing with other people," he says. "We show them

---

[5] Billy E. Vaughn, Ph.D., president and founder of The Diversity Training University International LLC, billy@diversityuintl.com, (858) 672-2654.

insight, and we show them practical activities to help them change their behavior. We teach inclusion. Everyone brings their own special differences into the workplace, and in companies that practice optimal inclusion, those differences are appreciated. Many organizations lag behind in their consciousness about inclusion, and it's no one's fault. It usually happens in an organization that's been successful in a particular area, and they're afraid if they change what they're doing, they'll lose ground in their success in areas of productivity and might lose their competitive edge."

✔ Checklist: Welcoming Cultural Diversity

❑ Tolerance toward people who don't look like you or have opinions like yours, regardless of your ethnicity, is the most important workplace value.

❑ The workplace is not a place for bias or prejudice. It's up to each person to practice patience, tolerance, and self-control to show respect to all people.

❑ Work is not the place to talk politics or religion. Do your best to allow people to have their thoughts and opinions without trying to convince them of yours.

❑ Work (or anyplace) is not the place for divisive behavior or insensitive language, regardless what nation you're from.

❑ Ask nicely about a person's nation of origin. Have them explain their foods, family system, and early education. Good communication fosters a happier and safer workplace with higher morale and helps diminish discrimination and harassment.

❑ If you are from another country and have become an American citizen, use language that includes other Americans. By continually using the word *we* or *our* or *my* as language meaning your home country, you create a separation between you and other Americans. For example, don't say, "We believe…," or "Our people think…," "My country…" unless you're referring to America.

Sexual Orientation Sensitivity in the Workplace

"Words can hurt, and words can bring people together," says Mark Abelsson,[6] a human relationship consultant in Los Angeles who specializes in sexual orientation, diversity, and sexual harassment issues in the workplace. "There are state laws and procedures in place in many states throughout the United States that protect gays and lesbians so they can safely disclose their sexual orientation in the workplace. While it's true that a company's policy can require someone to behave in a certain way even if they don't believe a certain way, a workplace that is inclusive is more productive for everybody. The Golden Rule should apply in all areas of the workplace. In order to respect ourselves, we all need to act respectfully to others."

✔ Checklist: Respecting Sexual Orientation

❑ Avoid the use of negative terms when referring to gay men or lesbian women. If you feel the need to label a person who is gay or lesbian when referring to them, say, "So & So is a gay man," or "So & So is a lesbian woman."

❑ Lesbian women call themselves either gay or lesbian. Honor their choice of terms.

❑ If it is necessary, and you need to describe whether or not an individual has announced sexual orientation to those at work, you may say, "So & So is an openly gay man," or "So & So is an openly lesbian woman."

❑ If an individual has not announced sexual orientation to those at work, respect his or her privacy and do not announce it. However, if a situation arises and you feel the need to tell people the individual is *not* open about sexual orientation, the correct term is, "So & So is closeted," or "So & So is not out."

❑ Do not use the term homosexual because it has a negative connotation among gays and lesbians.

---

[6] Mark Abelsson, (323) 222-1938, abelsson@earthlink.net.

❑ Do not use the term "gay lifestyle." It stereotypes gays and lesbians in a negative way. The term "gay lifestyle" has been used in political discourse to label all gay men as promiscuous, with deviant social behaviors. When referring to a group of individuals who are gay and lesbian, use the term "gay and lesbian community."

❑ Use the term "sexual orientation" and not "sexual preference."

❑ Attempt to use gender neutral terms. If you send an invitation to a company holiday party, avoid addressing the invitation, "So & So plus Spouse." If a person who is gay or lesbian receives such an invitation, he or she may not feel welcome to bring a partner. Instead, address the invitation, "So & So plus partner" or "So & So plus date" or "So & So plus one." This sends a message to individuals who are gay and lesbian (as well as heterosexual people) that all people are valued in the workplace, not just married, heterosexual people.

|||||||||||||||||||||||||||||||

CHAPTER SUMMARY

★ Be sensitive to people of all ethnic backgrounds, nationalities, religions, genders, or sexual orientations. If you find yourself feeling biased or acting biased toward anyone, find someone to talk to about your prejudice and learn to act in a more tolerant and patient way.

★ It's your problem when you are biased or judgmental toward any persons or groups of people, and you must resolve it.

★ Open channels of communication in the workplace help create a safe and harmonious atmosphere that is free of prejudice and division.

★ Words hurt. Use inclusive language without discriminating against anyone or any group of people.

Disability Sensitivity in the Workplace

THERE ARE MORE THAN 54 MILLION Americans with a disability. These individuals should be treated with the same respect and dignity afforded people who do not have disabilities. Patronizing behavior and use of incorrect language, such as "he's handicapped" or "she's disabled" is highly inappropriate in any setting. Americans with disabilities have made great strides over the past 20 years in the areas of education and building accessibility, yet there is still a perceived glass ceiling when it comes to advancement in the American workplace.

Kathie Snow[1] has become a collective voice for what is known as "people first language," which offers a distinct

---

[1] Kathie Snow, *Disability Is Natural: Revolutionary Common Sense for Raising Successful Children with Disabilities*, Brave Heart Press, www.disabilityisnatural.com.

vocabulary of inclusive language regarding people with disabilities. In addition to being an educator and author, she is also a wife and the proud mother of Emily and Benjamin. When Benjamin was four months old, he was diagnosed with cerebral palsy. It was then that Kathie became an educator and advocate to help promote inclusion for people with disabilities. Her intelligence, humor, and candor have helped her to educate the public about her important message. "Don't refer to those with disabilities by describing what a person *is*," Kathie advises. "For example, you wouldn't say, 'Melinda is a stroke victim.' If it's necessary to explain a person's condition, say what the person *has* by saying something like, 'Melinda has had a stroke.'"

Talking about a person's disability in a casual or business conversation is impolite and unnecessary. A disability is simply one of many aspects of an individual's personal characteristics and should never be used as a descriptor or definer. For example, you would find it impolite if your ongoing neck pain was a constant descriptor attached to your name.

The following words are considered dehumanizing and degrading to a person who has a disability: cripple, retarded, handicapped, defective, damaged, and invalid. Kathie Snow's people first language describes what a person has, not what a person is. Here are some examples that Kathie helped formulate:

Correct usage:	"Bill uses a wheelchair."
Incorrect usage:	"Bill is deformed [has no legs]."
Correct usage:	"Lisa has a visual impairment."
Incorrect usage:	"Lisa is almost blind." (However, many people with no sight prefer to be described as "blind" instead of as having a "visual impairment." When in doubt, ask the person which description she or he prefers.)
Correct usage:	"Lilly is a person of small stature."
Incorrect usage:	"Lilly is a dwarf or midget." (Some people prefer the term "little people." Ask which they prefer.)

Correct usage:	"Mark has an emotional disability."
Incorrect usage:	"Mark is emotionally disturbed [or crazy]."
Correct usage:	"Gene has a cognitive [or developmental] disability."
Incorrect usage:	"Gene is retarded."
Correct usage:	"Susan has a hearing impairment."
Incorrect usage:	"Susan is hearing impaired." (However, some people with no hearing prefer the term "deaf." When in doubt, ask the person which term is preferred.)
Correct usage:	"Phil uses a communication device."
Incorrect usage:	"Phil is mute."
Correct usage:	"Ann uses crutches [or a wheelchair or a walker]."
Incorrect usage:	"Ann is confined to a wheelchair" or "Ann is wheelchair-bound."

Correct	Incorrect
People with disabilities	The handicapped or disabled
He has a cognitive disability	He's mentally retarded
She has autism	She's autistic
He has Down's syndrome	He's Down's
She has a learning disability	She's learning-disabled
He has a physical disability	He's a quadriplegic/crippled
She's of short stature	She's a dwarf (or midget)
He has an emotional disability	He's emotionally disturbed
She uses a wheelchair or mobility chair	She's wheelchair bound
He receives special ed services	He's in special ed
Kids without disabilities	Normal or healthy kids
Congenital disability	Birth defect

Brain injury	Brain damaged
Accessible parking	Handicapped parking
She needs… or she uses…	She has a problem with…

In general conversations, use the term, "people who don't have disabilities," instead of "normal people" or "able-bodied people." These terms imply that people with disabilities are "abnormal" or "unable." If you're curious about a co-worker's disability, simply ask the person to tell you about it. Most people are more than willing to help you understand. They would rather give you the facts than have you believe false assumptions or inaccurate ideas. Simply say, "Could you tell me more about your disability?" Do not say, "What's wrong with you?" or "What happened to you?"

Suggestions for Working with a Person Who Has a Disability

- Before assisting a person with a disability, ask whether he or she needs your help. Do not assume you know how or when to help.
- When you are introduced to a person with a disability, shake hands. If the person offers you her or his left instead of right hand, shake that hand. In case the person is unable to shake hands, touch him or her lightly on the arm or shoulder to convey your greeting.
- Don't pet, feed, or distract a person's assistance dog. The dog is working, and it cannot perform its duties when it's paying attention to you.
- Before walking with a person who has a visual impairment, ask if she or he needs assistance. The person may need to hold on to your arm or elbow as a guide.
- When you are in a group of people that includes a person who has a visual impairment, state your name before speaking so he or she knows who is talking. When you leave the group say, "It's Mary. I'm leaving now."

- Do not lean on a person's wheelchair. Respect the chair as a part of the individual's personal space.
- Do not bring a mobility device (cane, walker, crutches) to a person unless you are asked to do so.
- When speaking at length with a person sitting in a wheelchair, find a chair and take a seat next to him or her so you're at the same eye level.
- Always speak directly to a person instead of to a companion. This applies even when the person has a sign language interpreter. Do not speak in a louder than normal voice unless requested to do so. Tell the person when you don't understand what he or she says and ask for the message to be repeated. Don't pretend you understood what was said when you didn't.
- Always presume the person with a disability is competent. Do not make assumptions or fall back on preconceived notions about what a person with a disability can or cannot do.

CHAPTER SUMMARY

★ Treat all people with respect and dignity.

★ When you must label a person's condition, explain what the person has and not what a person is. Say, "Melinda has had a stroke." Do not say, "Melinda is a stroke victim."

★ If you're curious about a person's disability, ask her or him to tell you about the condition.

★ Do not offer help to someone who has a disability unless the person asks for it.

ETHICS IN THE WORKPLACE

Personal Code of Ethics

I F YOU SUPPORT THE AMERICAN SYSTEM OF free enterprise, then it's your responsibility to stand tall, accept personal accountability, and do what you can to help our nation become strong. Perhaps it's a lofty goal, but if you are willing to examine and monitor your behavior and hold your standards high, American businesses will benefit from your commitment. Here is a suggested Personal Code of Ethics for you to consider following as a benchmark for your professional behavior. Read it, then consider signing and dating it as a standard and personal commitment to work toward in all your dealings.

Examine your company's mission statement and add your own commitments within your code of ethics so you'll be entirely congruent with the promises it's making to its customers. Be very clear about what your company is asking you to do so you can do your job with integrity and honesty.

Personal Code of Ethics for _____

Your name here

I agree to:

- Maintain the highest level of professional standards as an employee of my company and conduct myself with honesty and integrity at all times toward all people.
- Show respect for my work and contribution to my company and offer my best efforts every day by presenting pertinent, accurate, and objective information.
- Keep confidences about my company's business; I will avoid gossip and harsh criticism of others and consistently offer an attitude of understanding toward all people.
- Listen carefully and allow people to give me information without interrupting or arguing with them.
- Honor my company and its resources and not squander, steal, or damage its assets; and be punctual and honor the value of time.
- Accept responsibility for the duties that have been assigned to me to each day and collaborate with others in a spirit of teamwork to accomplish defined goals.
- Continually improve my skills as a person and as an employee through educational enhancement programs to perform my job in a timely way at a high level of excellence.
- Exhibit high moral character as an individual and not engage in any illegal behaviors that might reduce my value to the company in the eyes of my employer.
- Offer praise and encouragement to my co-workers when appropriate and be pleasant to people in my business dealings.

- Show respect to all people in the workplace and honor diversity in all areas including age, gender, disability, sexual orientation, ethnic background, nationality, and religion.

X _____   X _____

Your name and your company's name   Date of signing

|||||||||||||||||||||||||||||

CHAPTER SUMMARY

★ Personal accountability is key to business success and personal esteem.

★ A code of personal ethics involves honesty, respect, trust, communication, responsibility, teamwork, personal excellence, high morals, acts that foster encouragement, and diversity sensitivity.

Corporate Code
of Ethics

T HE MAGIC BUBBLE OF CORPORATE TRUST has burst, and it's been a very sober- ing time in corporate America since the beginning of the new century. It's been excruciatingly painful to watch the evening news and see highly revered cor- porate executives in handcuffs and with blank expressions on their faces being escorted to waiting police cars. It's as if all the batteries in all the calculators died at once, and no one wants to take the blame for the billion-dol- lar rounding errors that have shaken consumer confidence.

CBS reported in July 2002 the results of a poll that found that only one out of every four Americans believes the major- ity of corporate executives are honest. In light of this sobering

On October 31, 2002, a federal grand jury handed a 78-count indictment accusing Andrew Fastow (former chief financial officer for Enron) of money laundering and fraud. Each of the counts could result in a maximum penalty of 10 to 20 years in prison.

> According to a survey conducted by GradSchools.com, more than 80 percent of students planning to receive their MBA believe that programs need to be developed to create a greater emphasis in the area of ethics.
>
> —*CFO* MAGAZINE, "LEAVE THE CLUBS HOME," OCTOBER 2002

report, everyone is scrambling to find ways to recreate public trust.

Corporate ethics should be a true reflection of what's going on behind closed doors; they should be a mirrored reflection to the public of leadership that directs the company toward success or failure. Must companies prove their honesty and credibility to regain the trust and respect of their employees, customers and investors? The answer is an unequivocal and resounding YES. In many ways, we must start again at the beginning to create and publicize the basic rules of ethical standards that companies must follow in order to continue to build a fair and civilized society.

Advice from the Council of Better Business Bureaus Inc.: Establishing an Ethical Business

The Council of Better Business Bureaus Inc.[1] has been working diligently in the background of American businesses and encouraging voluntary self-regulation and consumer education

---

[1] The Council of Better Business Bureaus Inc. (CBBB) and the Better Business Bureau® (www.bbb.org) is supported by 250,000 local businesses throughout America and was founded in 1912. They have attracted 300 leading-edge national corporations among their leadership. The Better Business Bureau is dedicated to fostering fair and honest relationships between businesses and consumers, instilling consumer confidence, and contributing to an ethical business environment.

since 1912. It has always promoted ethical business standards to create consumer confidence and is to be lauded for its efforts. The following is their advice for establishing an ethical business:

> *Attention to ethics is on the rise in businesses across the country and many businesses are realizing that in order to succeed, they must earn the respect and confidence of their customers. The most significant factor in earning this respect and confidence is to act and conduct business in an ethical manner. Unethical business practices create ill-will among customers and the community, not only toward a particular business firm, but toward business as a whole.*
>
> *The Better Business Bureau offers the following suggestions to help you maintain a culture that sets high standards of behavior in buyer and seller relationships:*
>
> * *Treat your employees with respect and fairness.*
> * *Make certain that your ethics policy starts at the top level so that company management sets an important example for all employees. Effectively communicate ethics policies to all employees.*
> * *Make sure that your company conveys a clear, professional message, to external and internal publics, concerning the ethics of your organization and expectations you hold for your employees.*
> * *Establish a customer service program and train your employees accordingly.*
> * *Make sure the program covers basic expectations on everything from telephone courtesy to handling dissatisfied customers.*
> * *Recognize that customer complaints are an opportunity! They can provide your company with the chance to clear up a misunderstanding with a valued customer or identify a very real problem within your organization.*

* *Seek to treat each customer fairly, demonstrate sound business practices, and resolve disputes in a fair and expeditious manner.*
* *Make sure your advertising says what it means and mean what it says.*
* *Deceptive and misleading advertising will only hurt your business and your industry.*
* *Don't undervalue or overvalue your products or services; doing either could lead to unrealistic customer expectations.*
* *In order to help a potential customer make a more informed buying decision, be forthcoming with detailed information about your business, its product or service, and anything else deemed pertinent to the situation. A legitimate business should have nothing to hide, and if a customer thinks you are withholding information they need, they may go elsewhere.[2]*

Developing Your Company's Code of Ethics

Most American companies have a code of ethics they make public that responds to their vision and philosophy. Whether you're a Fortune 500 company, a small company, a group, or an association, formulate your own simple and direct code of ethics for your clients and customers to read that publicly states your business practices. For example, the Texas Independent Automotive Association[3] was created by a group of people who organized leaders in the automotive service industry in Texas to promote professionalism and quality service within their industry and

---

[2] "Establishing an Ethical Business," ©1995–2002. Council of Better Business Bureaus. Used by kind permission.

[3] The Texas Independent Automotive Association (www.tiaa.net) was founded in 1980.

offer a network of support for its members. The association has kindly allowed its straightforward, four-point Code of Ethics to be included here.

Code of Ethics for the Texas Independent Automotive Association

- We will perform professional, quality work at a fair price.
- We pledge to perform warranties quickly and cheerfully.
- We consider it our duty to advise our customers of any real or potentially dangerous condition observed while servicing their vehicles.
- We notify customers if completion promises cannot be fulfilled.

CHAPTER SUMMARY

★ Create a set of standards for ethical behavior in your company, business, group, or association.

Etiquette There, Then, and Now

History
of Etiquette

W E AMERICANS THINK WE'RE *SO* CIVI-lized and sophisticated, but it certainly puts things in perspective to realize that the table fork wasn't commonly used here until the 1900s. Forks began to appear on dining tables in parts of Europe and early colonial America during the 17th century. Before that, food was eaten with the hands and spoons. Forks were first used in a few kitchens to hold onto meat while carving it into bite-sized pieces before serving. Early spoons date back to prehistoric times and were carved from animal horns.

Etiquette wasn't made up by experts in a cultural think tank. Social manners have evolved over thousands of years; the earliest recorded use was by those in political and religious circles. As people gathered together in larger villages and cities, those in power began defining the rules of behavior, and basic decrees for etiquette were developed. Over time, those in the inner circles of power and privilege created more and more elaborate etiquette rituals to separate themselves from what they considered *the common classes.*

In light of the need for etiquette to create a civilized world, it has never been more important for people to act within certain parameters of predictable behavior so they can interact, communicate, and conduct business with one another. Therefore, manners, diplomacy, and etiquette will continue to evolve to meet the needs of contemporary society and business. Knowing the basic rules of conduct can help you to translate meanings and messages in verbal and nonverbal conversations. It also gives a decided advantage to those who possess this valuable information.

The notion of civilized behavior has evolved over the past 5,000 years. People have adapted to tenets for social order out of necessity and respect for various laws based on territorial landholdings, religious doctrine, commerce and trade, political power, and even regarding basic hygiene to help prevent the spread of disease.

Since the early days when this nation was formed, Americans have adopted many European codes of conduct as a basic template for civil and social order. Many social manners used today came from rules handed down orally within family structures from generation to generation. Ritual and ceremonial traditions became codified in the formal court of Louis XIV in the late 1600s and early 1700s in France.

As early American cities grew in the mid-1800s, people wanted to know how they should behave in public venues and so relied on English etiquette books to help educate themselves.

During the radical 1960s, the youth of America rebelled against the strict set of cultural norms that were set firmly in place in the 1950s; American life has never been the same since then. The 1960s spawned a new culture of proclaimed individualists who set their own personal codes of conduct and then designed lifestyles to accommodate those choices. The era since then has obviously not been without its problems; however, it has been a time of boundless creativity and imagination. Since those tumultuous years of relaxed standards, America has pushed the limits of experimentation with art, science, medicine, and education, and this birthed the era of technology that has changed the world.

Despite Americans' need to experience freedom of choice and demonstrate the inalienable right of expression, there are still benchmarks for manners in the American workplace that have provided underpinnings of our evolving society. Like all circles and cycles, contemporary culture is always looking for something to hold on to that will provide stability during rocky times. In light of consumer confidence and political troubles, it appears that people are searching for ways to hold on—to each other—and forge bonds of trust during uncertain times.

A Manners Time Line

The fascinating history of etiquette is a rich cultural study of the military, of national conflicts, philosophy, art, health and survival, class systems, religious practices, dining, commerce, and communication. Each era, each nation, and each culture since the beginning of recorded time has created its own standards for appropriate personal conduct. Out of these standards have come many of the manners people use today in both their personal lives and business practices.

> "A free society is a place where it's safe to be unpopular."
> —ADLAI STEVENSON, AMERICAN POLITICAL LEADER, 1900–1965

9th Century B.C.
The first recorded handshake was found in a stone relief. The carving depicts the king of Babylonian, Marduk-Zakir-Shumi, shaking hands with the king of Assyria, Shalmanasser III, as a symbolic gesture to transfer his godly powers. Later, the handshake became an act of good will.

Pope Gregory the Great instigated the use of the phrase
"God Bless You" when someone sneezed.
He used this phrase because the bubonic plague
was overtaking Rome.

6th Century A.D.

Pope Gregory the Great instigated the use of the phrase "God Bless You" for when someone sneezed. The bubonic plague (commonly referred to as The Black Death) was sweeping through Europe during his reign, and those who were infected with the plague sneezed and yawned spasmodically until they died.

The bubonic plague was also the inspiration for the following familiar children's nursery rhyme:

- *Ring around the rosy.* This refered to the swollen lymph nodes (buboes) that first appeared on those infected with bubonic plague. Buboes led to the term "boo-boos" for when a small child hurts themselves in minor accidents.
- *Pocket full of posey.* A small nose-bouquet of flowers that kept a person from smelling the plague-induced odor of rotting flesh.
- *Ashes, ashes.* Plague victims sneezed and spread their germs. "Ashes, ashes" became "a-choo" in common vocabulary.
- *All fall down!* Ninety percent of plague victims died. Some reports claim the 6th-century bubonic plague killed one third of the entire population of Europe.

12th–14th Century A.D.

Chivalry was born as an honored class system that was bestowed on the warriors called knights who served during the Crusades. The warriors embodied personal attributes such as honor, loyalty, and highly dignified behavior.

Knights lifted their face plates with their right hand
and kept them up at their right temple
during conversations.

Knights wore heavy metal armor to protect themselves in battle. When two met on horseback, they recognized each other by the elaborate, engraved artwork on their armor. The lower-ranking knight was the first to lift his heavy metal face plate as a gesture of respect and recognition. Knights lifted their face plates with their right hand and kept them up at their right temple during conversations. This gesture is still used today by soldiers greeting one another in all military armed forces; it's called saluting. The lower-ranking soldier is also still the first to salute a senior-ranking officer.

17th Century

The term "étiquette" is a French word that means *ticket* or *label*. Louis XIV's reign stabilized France as a country of great power in Europe. Those who attended court were given a "ticket," or list of the rules, so they would know how to conform to the proper conduct established by Louis XIV. This saved visitors from public humiliation before the king. Many of today's manners come from this significant time in French history.

Louis XIV started the trend of dulling the sharp
tip of table knives to reduce their use
as weapons during meals.

Louis XIV started the trend of dulling the sharp tip of table knives to reduce their use as weapons during meals.

In the 17th century, a young boy named George Washington transcribed the 110 *Rules for Civility* that were written by the French Jesuits in the 15th century. These 110 tenets became the bedrock of Washington's life; he used them while serving as the first president of the United States of America.

18th Century

As colonies in early America grew and people began to interact with others outside their primary family structures and church communities, they wanted to know how to behave in front of strangers in new situations. They sought out booklets and pamphlets that immigrants brought with them from England and other parts of Europe.

19th Century

The middle class emerged as a distinct and growing sector of the American population. Education and information became available to help people improve their social skills and elevate their status in society. As information about manners became common knowledge among all classes, they fell out of favor and were considered inconsequential compared to more pressing problems of the day.

Those who considered themselves "upper class" elevated their level of manners to higher ceremonies and rituals to separate themselves from the lower classes.

Families and individuals sought privacy for themselves for the first time. New homes for the average American family had separate rooms for sleeping. Until this time, the average home was one room, including the kitchen, and the toilet was outside in an outhouse.

20th Century

America's 48 contiguous states became formalized as a nation, called the United States of America, in 1912. The average life span in 1920 was 54 years.

The late 1960s ushered in an era of personal, social, and sexual experimentation and relaxed standards and codes of conduct. Americans divorced, and mothers entered the workforce to help care for their children. Casual dress and dining became the norm to accommodate busy lives.

Laws were written to protect employed American workers in the areas of age, religion, gender, ethnic origin, nationality, sexual orientation, sexual harassment, health and safety, fair pay and time off, losing or leaving a job, and privacy.

A 1996 *U.S. News & World Report* survey concluded that 89 percent of Americans believed that incivility was a serious problem in America; 91 percent of those surveyed said that they believed the decline of civility contributed to violence.

21st Century

Workplace fairness and civility have become major considerations for those in the profit and nonprofit sectors of American business. Acceptable codes of conduct are prime considerations for associations, corporations, educational systems, law enforcement, religious groups, real estate, private and professional organizations, unions, political parties, the technology and e-business sector, medical professionals, publishing, and the media.

Early in 2002, a report from Public Agenda[1] stated that 79 percent of those interviewed believe that lack of respect and courtesy are a serious problem in American society and that we should be addressing those issues. In 2002, many major American corporations were investigated for improper business practices.

CHAPTER SUMMARY

★ Etiquette was born out of rituals and rules involving social order, war, political structure, and basic hygiene.

★ Knowing and practicing the rules for contemporary business is an individual's responsibility.

---

[1] Public Agenda is a nonpartisan, nonprofit public opinion research and citizen education organization based in New York City. It was founded in 1975 by social scientist and author Daniel Yankelovich and former Secretary of State Cyrus Vance.

Global Etiquette

I N A GLOBAL ECONOMY, THERE IS AN INCREAS-ing need for countries to learn each other's basic cultural tenets for etiquette to help ease anxiety and increase effective communication during business deal-ings. Although this book is meant to instruct you on American business man-ners, this chapter offers you a snapshot into the unique codes of conduct for business in 12 different countries. It's up to you to learn what is expected of you as you prepare to travel to another country.

If your company invites people from other countries to visit your office in the United States, do your homework to learn about the country's codes of business conduct and try to accommodate them to make your visitors comfortable. Your efforts to be a gracious host will be rewarded with higher levels of rapport and trust during your business negotiations.

As you examine the various rules of business conduct in other countries, you'll quickly see how their rich traditions are based on thousands of years of practice. America is a young country by comparison, and many of our business practices are considered impetuous and brazen to people from other countries. In fact, it would be a mistake to assume you can travel to any country outside the United States and conduct business as you would here. Please refer to the reading list in the back of this book for references regarding business travel in a variety of countries.

|||||||||||||||||||||||||||||||||||||||||||||||||||||||||||||||||||||||||||||||||||||||||||||||||||||||||||||||||||||||||||||||||||||

Don't expect the rest of the world to comply with America's fast-paced mind-set.

|||||||||||||||||||||||||||||||||||||||||||||||||||||||||||||||||||||||||||||||||||||||||||||||||||||||||||||||||||||||||||||||||||||

Every country has its own standards for greetings, introductions, dining, business card exchange, small talk, relationship building, punctuality, gift giving, negotiations, and conversation. While foreign business travel does not require that you know all the subtleties of a country's culture, you are expected to show respect and comply with basic tenets for behavior. The more information you have ahead of time, the more successful your business dealings are likely to be.

Many Americans have failed in business dealings abroad and with people from other cultures doing business within America because they were unaware and unprepared for the cultural differences and social amenities they faced. For example, Americans are always ready to close the deal, even during the first sales call on a potential client. Don't expect the rest of the world to comply with America's fast-paced mind-set. Expect your business dealings abroad to go slowly and plan to take your time and build relationships based on trust. Get to know people and allow them to get to know you before you begin to ask for their business cooperation.

> "Though we travel the world over to find the beautiful, we must carry it with us or we find it not."
> —Ralph Waldo Emerson, PHILOSOPHER AND POET, 1803–1882

When You're in Japan

- The Japanese are gracious people and will shake your hand when they meet you since you are a Westerner; watch closely, and you may also see them bow slightly.
- The Japanese will introduce the most important person in the room first. Next, they will introduce you to those people in the meeting with less important ranks and titles. Do your best, just as you would in all countries, to pronounce their names correctly; ask for help if necessary. No one anywhere in the world likes to hear her or his name mispronounced.
- Keep your arms uncrossed when a person is speaking to you.
- Bowing is acceptable for a Westerner. When doing it to a person with a higher-ranking title than yours, bow slightly lower than they do and hold your bow longer to show you respect the person and his or her rank. Lower your eyes as you bow and place each of your hands on the outside of your thighs with your palms open. If you rise from your bow and the other person has not yet risen, bow again.
- Present your business card to a Japanese associate after your introduction. Do it with both hands with the type facing up, toward the recipient, so they can read it. Have the reverse side of your card printed in Japanese in case your recipients do not speak English.
- Hand your card first to the person in the room with the highest rank. Then give it to those with lesser rank in order of importance.

When You're in Hong Kong

- The traditional Western handshake is common in Hong Kong; however, people there may also offer you a slight bow.

- As in Japan, offer and receive your business card (following introductions) with both hands. Study and handle a card given to you to very carefully to indicate your respect for the other person.
- Although English is widely spoken in Hong Kong, Cantonese is the second most common language, and you may choose to have the reverse of your businesses card printed in this dialect.
- Expect your business to move slowly and do your best to avoid discussing anything unpleasant in public.
- When you take a break from eating rice, lay your chopsticks down flat next to your bowl instead of letting them stick up in the rice bowl like a flagpole.
- The Chinese are very private people. Avoid asking questions of a personal nature.

When You're in India

- It is acceptable in India to present your business card after introductions have been made. Since most Indians speak English, it is not necessary to print the reverse side in another language.
- Indians value title and rank. Employees of Indian-based companies can be expected to strictly follow the rules of their employers. When dealing with businesses in India, you will receive orders only from company leaders.
- Business negotiations can be long and detail-driven. Indians will not be rushed into making decisions before they're ready. You should make a habit of writing everything down and being clear about all your agreements during the long discussions and negotiations.
- Show utmost respect for religious traditions.
- When dining, eat only with your right hand. Your left hand is considered unclean.

When You're in Thailand

- Although Thais will shake the hands of Westerners, it's wise to learn their form of greeting. It resembles a prayer stance offered with a slight bow. Fold your hands together as if you are praying and hold them close to the middle of your chest. Keep them there when greeting your peers, but raise them to the bridge of your nose when you greet an older person or a Buddhist monk as a sign of respect.

- Find a printer to print the back of your business card in Thai.
- Relationships are important to the Thai people. If they like and trust you, you have a greater chance of doing business with them. If they don't like and trust you, your efforts will stall before your negotiations ever begin.
- Those in authoritative positions expect to be shown respect for their rank. Although you should show all people respect, be sure to make overt demonstrations to those in leadership roles.
- As a Westerner, you must learn to minimize your emotions. Present yourself as a calm and experienced professional in all your business dealings.
- Thais consider the tops of their heads highly sacred parts of the human body. Never touch the top of your head or that of anyone else's. They also believe the foot is the least sacred part of the human body. Never point the bottom of your foot at anyone as this gesture is considered an insult.

When You're in Argentina

- Argentine people are warm and gracious, but don't let that fool you. They must like and trust you before they'll ever consider doing business with you. They must also see that you're a person who is honorable and dependable before beginning any negotiations.
- Although the Argentines are formal in their business dealings, they enjoy a sincere and enthusiastic handshake.
- Offer your business card following the initial introductions and handshakes. Although many Argentines speak English, it's a good idea to print the reverse of your card in Spanish.

- There's a double standard for punctuality in Argentina. While they expect you to be punctual for a meal or meeting, your host may be late. Be patient and don't comment on his or her tardiness.

When You're in France

- Don't use a firm Western handshake in France, or people will consider you pushy. The French handshake consists of one brief hand pump in a light grip.
- Exchange business cards with French associates following handshakes and introductions. It is wise to print the reverse side of your card in French.
- You will often see the French offer kisses on both cheeks when greeting one another. However, that greeting is used only between close friends and family members, not in normal business greetings.
- Before leaving on your trip, learn to speak a few words of French. Your efforts will pay off. In case you don't have time to do this and your business dealings are important, hire an interpreter to help you before, during, and after your meetings.
- Expect your negotiations to take time and plan to make several trips to France before an agreement is reached.
- Use people's last names preceded by Monsieur (Mr.) or Madame (Mrs.). Avoid using first names unless invited to do so.

When You're in Germany

- Punctuality is expected in all your dealings with Germans.
- In many parts of Germany, rapping one's knuckles on the table is a substitute for handshakes at the beginning and at the end of the meeting when many people are present. Knuckle rapping is also a way of showing applause or agreement.
- Germans want to know who you are when they are dealing with you. Feel free to talk about your education, rank,

title, and affiliations during introductions and conversations. You may even list them on your business card.

- The Germans use formal titles in business. Don't use someone's first name unless invited to do so. Refer to them as Herr (Mr.) or Frau (Mrs.) followed by last name.

- Prepare, prepare, prepare. The Germans are meticulous about their business dealings and will question you about every detail of a proposal. Your business relationship and negotiations will suffer unless you know the answers to their questions.

- Don't ever assume you have total agreement for your business proposal until you have a signed contract. After that, be prepared to deliver exactly what you said you would.

When You're in Italy

- Italians enjoy the handshake and use it often during a business day. If you're a man, don't be surprised if you're embraced by another man, but don't initiate the embrace yourself.

- Learn to speak some Italian before you leave home. You might also want to hire a translator before, during, and after your business meeting for vital negotiations.

- Take great care to prepare appealing and artistic business proposals. Create packages and letters that will appeal to the Italian sense of visual appreciation and beauty.

- Italians have a long history of respect for rank and title. Always make sure you know who is the highest-ranking official in the room; this person has the most power in all your dealings, and you should defer to them.

- When speaking or writing to your Italian associates, use the salutations Signore (Mr.) or Signora (Mrs.) followed by last name. Always use titles for those who have them. Don't use anyone's first name unless invited to do so.

- Be sensitive to the fact that the Catholic Church is an important part of life for Italian people.

When You're in Saudi Arabia

- Print your business card with English on one side and Arabic on the other.
- Shake hands with your right hand only.
- When dining, use only your right hand.
- Expect your business dealings to take place in groups and avoid asking for private meetings. If someone wants a private meeting, he or she will ask for one.
- It is polite to accept the offer of coffee or sweet tea when it is offered. Your host will be pleased if you agree to drink a second cup.
- Business takes into consideration the tenets of the Islamic faith.
- Always ask before taking photographs of Saudis.
- The family is all-important. It is polite to ask about the health and happiness of male members but never mention the women.
- Don't expect to talk about business during meals. Dining is a time of quiet and relaxation.

When You're in China

- Since China's leadership is part of the Communist party, don't expect your business negotiations to go easily. Westerners and their ideas are not easily welcomed into this culture.
- The Chinese will shake hands with Americans, but you should wait for them to do so. They also generally give a slight bow from the shoulders (not the waist). Or they may only bow their head by making a quick nod in your direction.
- Expect your Chinese associates to stand very close to you. If you back up, they will move with you.

- Bring plenty of business cards, preferably printed in gold ink. Print English on one side and the local Chinese dialect (such as Mandarin) on the other.
- Be gracious when given a compliment but deny that you deserve any praise. Humility is a highly-valued virtue in China.
- The Chinese are punctual and expect you to be, too.
- Be aware that when a group of business leaders enters a room, the most important person enters first.
- The Chinese are interested in dealing only with decision-makers in your company.
- Do not go to China expecting to present and finalize your proposal. The Chinese will go through long negotiations before reaching a decision.

When You're in England

- Contrary to what you might think, the British do not conduct business like Americans. They are slower to act on decisions and prefer to make gradual changes rather than major and abrupt moves.
- Conserve your emotions and present yourself as a seasoned business professional capable of understanding the needs of the British.
- Formality is key when setting and confirming your appointments. Use your best professional manners to assure your British associates that you're pleased they've agreed to meet with you. Confirm your appointment ahead of time and once again, assure them you're looking forward to your meeting.
- Always use the formal address of Mr., Mrs., or Miss. Do not use first names unless invited to do so.
- Avoid using American jargon or slang. It is best to use full sentences with proper grammar.
- Try not to tell stories about yourself that could make you look too emotional or untrustworthy.

When You're in Mexico

- When preparing for your business in Mexico, learn to speak some Spanish. Many people in major cities speak English, but those in smaller towns and villages usually don't. If you do not learn to speak some Spanish, take an interpreter with you to help before, during, and after your meetings.
- Have your business cards printed in English on one side and Spanish on the other.
- Mexicans have a more relaxed sense of time than Americans. It is always best to arrive on time for your meetings, but you may have to wait for your associates. Don't mention their tardiness when this happens.
- When addressing Mexican people, use Señor (Mr.) and Señora (Mrs.) followed by their last name. When you don't know a woman's marital status, address her as Señorita (Miss) followed by her last name.
- Mexicans enjoy a warm, enthusiastic handshake. If you are well liked, you may also receive a gentle cupping of your elbow as a warm addition. It is best if you do not initiate this elbow cupping.

||||||||||||||||||||||||||||||||||||

CHAPTER SUMMARY

- ★ In Japan, offer a slight bow when shaking hands.
- ★ In Hong Kong, consider printing the reverse of your business card in Cantonese.
- ★ In India, you will receive orders from company leaders.
- ★ In Thailand, present yourself as a calm and experienced professional.
- ★ In Argentina, you must be trusted and respected before you can conduct business.
- ★ In France, avoid a firm handshake or you will be labeled as pushy.

★ In Germany, you are expected to be fully prepared and knowledgeable about your business

★ In Italy, defer to the highest-ranking person in the room.

★ In Saudi Arabia, expect your meetings to take place in groups.

★ In China, print your business cards in gold ink.

★ In England, use your best professional manners for conducting business.

★ In Mexico, if you're well-liked, you may receive an elbow cupping with a handshake.

A Note from the Author

IT IS WITH GREAT HUMILITY THAT I SAY, "THANK YOU FOR SHARING your time with me." I began planning this book long before I actually began to write it. I've been teaching this work for more than 25 years with the dedicated passion of someone who loves the energy and buzz of American business. Over the course of my professional career, I've wined and dined with the captains of industry and the barons and baronesses of big business, and taken tea with politicians and potentates all over the world.

Many people have asked me over the years, "Phyllis, are successful people really that different from the rest of us? Or, are they just lucky?" The answer is, "Yes. They *really are* that different." I wrote this book to let you know *how* they're different so you can emulate their strategies and become equally successful.

Successful people know the rules of decorum and are more productive. Their self-esteem is high, and they are consistently productive since they don't waste time or energy second-guessing themselves in the normal course of a day. They face challenges with confidence in a way that says to the world, "Gimme' the ball."

May your days ahead be successful, abundant, and filled with the joys and opportunities of those granted the privilege of working in American business.

Warmest Sincere Regards,
Phyllis Davis

To Contact Phyllis Davis about Speaking to Your Company or Group

Please refer to www.mycoach.com for information on having Phyllis Davis speak or give training for your company or group, conference, association meeting, or corporate retreat. She enjoys speaking about the subject she loves the most: American business etiquette and ethics. She welcomes your call.

If You'd Like to Become Certified to Teach Phyllis Davis' Material, Join Her Association, American Business Etiquette Trainers Association (ABETA)

You can become certified to teach this work to your company, businesses or social groups, associations, conventions and conferences, corporate retreats, and academic environments. Go to www.mycoach.com for more information. In three days of training, you'll become certified in American Business Etiquette Trainers Association (ABETA) and learn everything you need to know to teach this work nationally or internationally. If you offer your speaking and training services for a fee, ABETA invites you to keep 100 percent of the money you make from your efforts after certification.

Suggested Reading List

Letitia Baldridge. *New Complete Guide to Executive Manners.* New York: Simon and Schuster, 1984.

Marcus Buckingham and Curt Coffman. *First Break All the Rules.* New York: Simon & Schuster, 1999.

Madelyn Burley-Allen. *Listening: The Forgotten Skill (A Self-Teaching Guide).* Hoboken, NJ: John Wiley & Sons, 1995.

Julia Cameron and Mark Bryan. *The Artist's Way.* New York: J.B. Tarcher, 10th edition, 2002.

Dale Carnegie. *How to Win Friends and Influence People.* New York: Pocket Books, reissue, 1994.

Cathy A. Costantino. *Designing Conflict Management Systems: A Guide to Creating Productive and Healthy Organizations.* San Francisco: Jossey-Bass, 1995.

Taylor, Cox Jr., Paul H. O'Neill, Robert E. Quinn, Jr., and Taylor Cox. *Creating the Multicultural Organization: A Strategy for Capturing the Power of Diversity.* Hoboken, N.J.: John Wiley & Sons, 2001.

Lillian Glass. *I Know What You're Thinking: Using the Four Codes of Reading People to Improve Your Life.* Hoboken, NJ: John Wiley & Sons, 2002.

Barbara G. Madonik. *I Hear What You Say, But What Are You Telling Me?: The Strategic Use of Nonverbal Communication in Mediation.* San Francisco: Jossey-Bass, 2001.

Judith Martin. *Miss Manners' Basic Training: Eating.* New York: Crown Publishing, 1997.

David Molden. *NLP Masterclass.* Saddle River, NJ: Financial Times Prentice Hall, December 15, 2000.

Terri Morrison, Wayne Conaway, and Joseph J. Douress. *Dunn & Bradstreet's Guide to Doing Business Around the World.* Saddle River, NJ: Prentice Hall/Career and Personal Development, 1997.

Terri Morrison, Wayne A. Conaway, George A. Borden, and Hans Koehler. *Kiss, Bow, or Shake Hands: How to Do Business in 60 Countries.* Hallbrook, MA: Adams Media Corp., 1995.

Peggy Post. *Emily Post's Etiquette* (16th Edition). New York: HarperCollins, 1997.

Tristine Rainer. *The New Diary: How to Use a Journal for Self-Guidance and Expanded Creativity.* New York: J. P. Tarcher, 1979.

William Sonnenschein and Arthur H. Bell. *The Diversity Toolkit: How You Can Build and Benefit from a Diverse Workforce.* Contemporary Books, 1999.

Albert J. Valentino. *Personality Selling: Using NLP and the Enneagram to Understand People and How They Are Influenced.* Iselin, NJ: Vantage Point, 1999.

Gordon Wainwright. *Teach Yourself Body Language.* New York: McGraw Hill—NTC, 2001.

Index

A

Abelsson, Mark, 211

Abusive criticism, dealing with, 135–136

Accountability, personal, 3, 129–142, 221–223

Active listening formula, 31–35

Agree and redirect, 120–121

Al-Anon program, 91

Allies, praising and respecting your, 118–120

American Business Etiquette Trainers Association (ABETA), 254

American workers, laws enacted to protect, 239

Anger, dealing with your, 138–140

Appointment
greeting, content and follow-up, codes of conduct for, 176–178
setting, codes of conduct for, 172–173

Argentina, doing business in, 245–246

Aristotle, 17, 109

Article writing for in-house newsletter, 93

Auditory
communicators, 41, 43, 46
digital communicators, 41, 44–45

B

Bad habits, feedback on your own, 97

Balaban, Melissa, 205–206

Barnum, P.T., 146
Bennett, Georgette, 206
Better Business Bureau advice
    for establishing an ethical
    business, 226–228
Bluntness, avoiding, 102–103
Bonaparte, Napoleon, 148
Brevity, 113
Brillat-Savarin, Jean
    Anthelme, 180
Bubonic plague, 236
Buck, Pearl, 115
Buddha, 138
Building bridges with ene-
    mies, 117–118
Bush, George W., 87, 207
Business card, 17–22
    exchange, 21
    presenting your, 18–20
    receiving a, 20–21
    seven most important
        items on your, 18
    use and purposes of the, 18
Business dinner
    choreographing, as host,
        179–186
    dressing for a, 187–188
    etiquette if you are the
        guest, 186–187
Business entrances, 11–16
Business image consultants,
    58, 64
Business meetings, 105–114
    checklist for attending,
        113–114
    leading a successful, 106–112

Business-casual dress
    for men, components of,
        64–70
    for women, components of,
        58–60

C
Carlyle, Thomas, 98
Carnegie, Dale, 40, 147
Cell phone manners, 167–170
China, doing business in,
    248–249
Chivalry of knights during the
    Crusades, 236–237
Churchill, Winston, 23, 105
Cicero, 113
Client protocol, 171–178
Code of a good meeting
    leader, 112
Code of ethics
    corporate, 4, 225–229
    personal, 4, 221–223
    Texas Independent
        Automotive
        Association's, 229
Cole, Rodney, 64
Colonial Americans, 238
Communication
    skills, 39–46
    the four channels of basic,
        40
    vs. bluntness, 103–104
Compliments
    behaviors that encourage,
        132–133
    behaviors that kill, 131–132
    delivering, 130, 132

receiving, 131, 132

Conference, convention or banquet, planning for and attending, 196–199

Confidential information, 124

Consumer
confidence, restoring, 4
loyalty, 129

Corporate
archaeology, 84–87
charity work, volunteering for, 92, 93
code of ethics, 225–229
corruption, 4, 226
executives, lack of public trust in, 225–226
ladder, moving up the, 83–94
politics, mastering, 115–128

Criticism, handling, 133–136

Cubicles, creating goodwill among inhabitants of office, 95–97

Cultural diversity in the workplace, welcoming, 210

D

Davis, Colle, 208

Death of a coworker, conduct in aftermath of, 99–100

Decisive action, 124–125

Decorating personal office space, 51–53

Diplomacy, 129–142
dictionary definition of, 39

skills, highlighting your, 92–94

Disability, workplace sensitivity toward, 213–217

Disney, Walt, 137

Diversity, workplace, 205–212

Dress codes of various industries, 57–58, 63–64

Durant, Will, 102

E

e-mail etiquette, 160–164

Effective
communication, benefits of, 40
listening, benefits of, 34

Einstein, Albert, 137

Eisenhower, Dwight D., 84, 107

Elevator pitch, 150–151

Emerson, Ralph Waldo, 11

Encouragement, offering, 127–128

Enemies into allies, 116–118, 130

England, doing business in, 249

Enron scandal, 226

Epictetus, 35

Ethics, need for more emphasis upon in MBA programs, 226. See also Code of ethics

Ethnic sensitivity in the workplace, 209–210

Excellence, habit of, 17

Expertise, sharing your, 93–94

F

Fastow, Andrew, 226
Faulkner, William, 178
Fax etiquette, 160, 164–5
Federal Communications
    Commission fine for com-
    pany initiating "junk faxes,"
    160
First impression, making a
    memorable, 13–16
Follow-up, networking,
    155–157
Ford, Henry, 194
Formal introductions in vari-
    ous institutions, 24
Fox, Dr. Emmet, 133
France, doing business in,
    246
Frustration, dealing with your,
    138–140
Funeral etiquette, 99–100

G

Game plan, creating your,
    85–87
Germany, doing business in,
    246–247
Getting the job, 73–79
Gift giving, business, 190–193,
    195
Global etiquette, 241–251
Goals, employee, 3
Goethe, 131
Golden rule of the workplace,
    206, 211
Goldsmith, Oliver, 51
Gossip, office, 140–142

H

Habit of excellence, 17
Handshake
    effecting an unmemorable
        business, 5–10
    first recorded, 235
Heroditus, 189
Hierarchy, importance of in
    business introductions,
    24–29
History
    and philosophy, knowing
        your company's,
        126–127
    of etiquette, 233–239
Hold button etiquette,
    166–167
Hong Kong, doing business
    in, 243–244
Honor, showing, 116–117
Humanity, highlighting your,
    93
Humor, workplace, 136–137

I

Image, business woman's,
    56–63
Improper business practices,
    American corporations
    investigated for, 239
Incivility seen as serious prob-
    lem and contribution to
    societal violence, 239
India, doing business in, 244
Internal networking, 83–94
Interoffice criticism, dealing
    with, 134–135

Interview
  steps for successful job,
    75–77
  tips from international
    Fortune 500 staffing
    manager, 77–79
Interviewer, creating positive
  chemistry with, 74
Introductions, business
  awkward moments in, 27
  making, 23–29
  ten rules for, 24–26
Irritating behaviors, dealing
  with, 96–97
Italy, doing business in,
  247–248

J

Japan, doing business in, 243
Job interview scenario, 75–77
Joke telling, workplace,
  136–137
Joyce, James, 24

K

Kennedy, John Fitzgerald, 241
Kettering, Charles F., 88
Kinesthetic communicators,
  41, 42–43, 45
Kirkegaard, Soren, 95
Kroc, Raymond Albert, 85

L

Leading successful business
  meetings, techniques for,
  106–112
Levity in the workplace, using
  quotations for, 137

Lincoln, Abraham, 221
Listening and hearing skills,
  31–38
Lord Stowell, 180
Louis XIV and origin of "eti-
  quette," 237
Loyalty, company, 125–126

M

Making an entrance, 11–16
Mann, Horace, 173
Manners "time line," 235–239
Martin Luther, 4
Maysonave, Sherry, 58
McDonald's founder, 85
McElroy, Leesa, 77
Mead, Margaret, 206
Meals, small talk during busi-
  ness, 48
Meetings, business, 105–114
Meister Eckhart, 31
Menninger, Karl, 34
Mexico, doing business in, 250
Middle-class, emergence of in
  19th Century America, 238
Mirroring, 14–16
Morley, Christopher, 83
Moving up the corporate lad-
  der, 83–94

N

Network, good reasons to,
  146–148
Networking, 145–157
  campaign, ninety day,
    146–148
  follow-up, 155–157

group meeting, four secret keys for attending, 148–149

plan, creating a successful, 149–150

Nietzsche, Friedrich, 155

O

Office
décor, 51–53
party etiquette, 193–196
politics, ten steps for winning at, 116–128
protocol and diplomacy for difficult and/or sensitive circumstances, 95–104

P

Pager/beeper manners, 169–170

Patton, General George, 137

Penney, J.C., 3

People First Language, 213–216

Personal
code of ethics, example of, 221–223
gestures, building relationship through, 120
phone calls during work hours, managing, 101
visibility campaign, 88–91

Pings, 120

Plato, 187

Pomerantz, Fran, 74–75

Pope
Gregory the Great, 236

office of, 23–24

Praise, how and when to give, 130–131

Private professional, remaining a, 122–123

Privileged information, safeguarding, 123–124

Professional appearance, 55–72
businessman's, 63–70, 71–72
businesswoman's, 56–63, 70–71

Profile, raising your, 92

Publicity campaign, personal, 92–94

Punctuality, codes of conduct for, 173–174

Q

Queen Victoria, 176

R

Reading list, suggested, 255–256

Recreational activities, participating in company, 93

Relationship management as core of office politics, 116. See also Office politics

Religious sensitivity in the workplace, 206–207

Resume, creating a professional, 79

Rickover, Navy Admiral Hyman G., 141

Roosevelt, Franklin, 23

Roosevelt, Theodore, 193
RSVP, 193

S

Sarcastic people, dealing with, 97–98
Saudi Arabia, doing business in, 248
Schweitzer, Albert, 136
Seamless entries, 12–13
Selective hearing, correcting, 34–35
Self-control, 138–140
Senior-ranking officer, making a favorable impression upon, 13–16
Sexual orientation in the workplace, respecting, 211–212
Shakespeare, William, 47
Sir Francis Bacon, 73
Small talk
    30-Day Rule, 48–50
    during business meals, 48, 183
    in business settings, 47–51, 53
    telephone, 50
Sneezing, origin of "God Bless You" when, 236
Snow, Kathie, 213–214
Social events, business-related, 194–196
Socrates, 92
Soft skills, employing to raise personal profile, 87–88, 146
Soldier's salute, history of, 237

Stevenson, Adlai, 235
Success, strategy for, 87
Sun Tzu, 130
Swift, Jonathan, 179

T

Technological etiquette, 159–170
Telephone
    manners, 101, 165–167
    small talk, 50
Texas Independent Automotive Association's Code of Ethics, 229
Thailand, doing business in, 244–245
Thoreau, Henry David, 55
Thurber, James, 171
Tolsoy, Leo, 101
Truman, Harry S., 233
Twain, Mark, 129

V

Vaughn, Billy E., 209–210
Visual communicators, 41, 42, 45
Voice-mail manners, 165–167
Voltaire, 42
Volunteer work, 92, 93

W

Waiting room, codes of conduct for, 174–175
Wardrobe as career investment, 57, 63
Washington, George, 225
    and his 110 Rules for Civility, 237–238

Wedding, proper manners at business associate's, 199–201

Williams, Tennessee, 150

Wirth, Linda, 207–208

Women in the workplace
business-casual dress, 58–60
gender sensitivity toward, 207–208
history of their entry into, 238–239

Image of, 56–63
respect for, 208–209

Working the room at a networking event, 150–154

Workplace fairness and civility in American business, 239

Wright, Frank Lloyd, 195

Y

Yawning in the workplace, 101–102

Young, Owen D., 159